Basic Physics Questions for GCSE

National Curriculum Edition

Bernard Abrams
MA CChem MRSC FRAS

ADT College, London

Stanley Thornes (Publishers) Ltd

First published in 1994 by
Stanley Thornes (Publishers) Ltd
Ellenborough House
Wellington Street
CHELTENHAM GL50 1YD
England

A catalogue record for this book is available from the British Library.

ISBN 0–7487–1724–2

Typeset by Tech-Set, Gateshead, Tyne & Wear.
Printed and bound in Great Britain at The Bath Press, Avon.

Contents

Preface to the National Curriculum Edition

Physical science surrounds us at all times, yet pupils can remain unaware of the relevance of the subject and often find tests and examinations difficult as a result. By using a wide variety of question styles and contexts, I hope that pupils will gain confidence as well as knowledge and understanding by working through the questions.

The pressures on a teacher's time are considerable and increasing. There is a constant demand for exercises that are effective, stimulating and also relatively easy to correct and evaluate.

This book has been written and more recently revised to help reinforce a basic understanding of Physical Science in both double award at GCSE and Science: Physics within the framework of the National Curriculum.

The specific aims of this question book are as follows:

1. To provide a framework within which pupils can compile a useful set of correct notes by working through and completing the various assignments, either on their own or with the help of the teacher.
2. To develop a pupil-centred approach to learning.
3. To provide an opportunity to develop pupil skills in numeracy and literacy.
4. To provide stimulating and varied material which can reinforce and consolidate the basic physics facts needed for Key Stage 4, whether in tests or in homework or classwork assignments. It can also, of course, be used as a revision programme.
5. To provide material that can be useful to students independently studying physics.
6. To develop scientific skills such as observation, measurement, interpretation and application.
7. To provide graded material that can be used in a mixed-ability or streamed class, so that all pupils will achieve some degree of success.
8. To provide material that is easy to use, easy to mark, and can be used in a wide variety of different ways by the teacher.

This National Curriculum edition contains up-to-date material relating to all the major areas of physics. It also includes a selection of questions specific to various extension topics.

Anticipating the difficulty some pupils may have with diagrams, I have simplified many of those essential to syllabuses. Although there are questions asking pupils to copy diagrams I expect that in many cases they will be traced.

Bernard Abrams,
ADT College, London, 1994

Acknowledgements

The author and publisher are grateful to Pan Books and Ian Ward for permission to use the extracts on pp. 179 and 185 respectively, and to the following for permission to reproduce examination questions:

London East Anglian Group

Midland Examining Group

Northern Examining Association

Southern Examining Group

Welsh Joint Education Committee

Many people have helped in the production of this book, and I would like to thank colleagues for their constructive criticisms of the questions. Finally it is my pleasure to thank the publishers Stanley Thornes, and all those involved in the design and production of this book.

Every effort has been made to contact copyright holders, and I apologise to any I have not been able to reach.

Theme 1

Matter

1 THE KINETIC MODEL

Particles

1 The diagrams on the left below show what happens to an ice cube as it is heated using a Bunsen burner. The diagrams on the right show what happens to the particles (molecules) during heating, but the order has been changed.

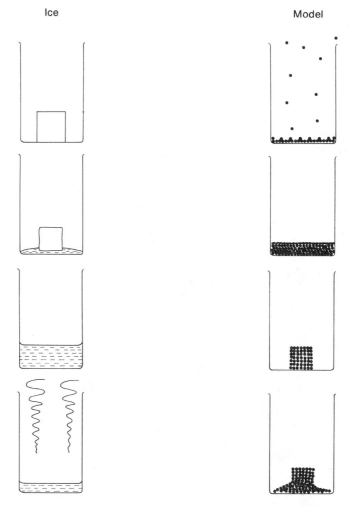

Ice   Model

a) i)   Copy the ice diagrams in the same sequence.

   ii) Draw the correct model next to each ice diagram.

b) As the liquid water changes to water vapour, the temperature remains constant. Explain what happens to the energy provided by the Bunsen burner.

2 The diagrams below show the arrangement of atoms in a metal block at room temperature (298 K, 25 °C) and at 398 K (125 °C). The atoms are vibrating about their average positions.

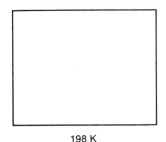

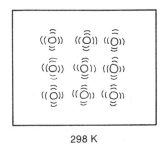

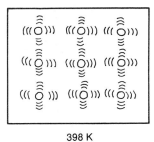

198 K   298 K   398 K

Re-draw the sequence of diagrams, adding the arrangement of particles you would expect at 198 K (−75 °C) in a way which shows:

a) the change in motion expected at this temperature

b) whether the sample has expanded or contracted compared to the situation at room temperature

Label the diagrams to indicate what they show.

3 The following diagrams represent the arrangement of particles in a solid, a liquid and a gas:

SOLID   LIQUID   GAS

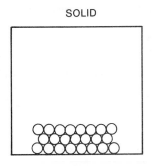

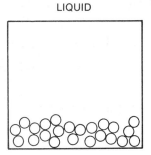

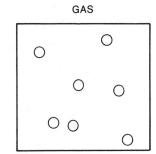

a) Referring to the diagrams, explain why gases can be compressed easily but solids and liquids cannot.

b) Why does a bicycle with air-filled rubber tyres give a smoother ride than one with solid rubber tyres?

4 The diagram below, which is not to scale, shows the atoms in a block of a solid material. A load is resting on the surface of the block.

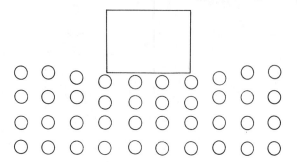

a) What holds the atoms together in a solid?

b) How does the solid support the weight of the load?

c) What would happen if the weight of the load was increased continuously?

Properties of Matter

1 All matter contains invisibly small particles. Explain each of the following situations by discussing the behaviour of these particles.

a) Small pieces of smoke, which appear as bright dots in a smoke cell viewed under a microscope, jiggle about a lot as they move.

b) Bromine vapour takes several minutes to diffuse through a container full of air, yet fills the container in a fraction of a second if the container has been evacuated beforehand.

c) A balloon inflates when air is pumped inside.

d) If a tin can with a tight-fitting lid is heated, the lid suddenly shoots off at high speed.

e) A metal rod expands when heated.

2 a) i) Stephen drops a stinkbomb in the corner of the classroom. Explain why it will very soon be smelt at the other side of the room.

ii) Why will the smell eventually disappear?

b) Meena carefully placed a single crystal of potassium permanganate (a soluble, purple compound) at the bottom of a beaker of water. The beaker was then left undisturbed for several days. What would she see on returning to the experiment? Explain what happened.

3 Copy and complete the following table to show, for each quantity listed:

a) the units in which the quantity is measured

b) a definition of the quantity.

Quantity	Unit	Definition
Density		
Specific heat capacity		
Latent heat of fusion		
Latent heat of vaporisation		
Tensile strength		
Hardness		

2 PHYSICAL CHANGES

Types of Change

1   The diagrams below represent particles of three substances which are undergoing changes:

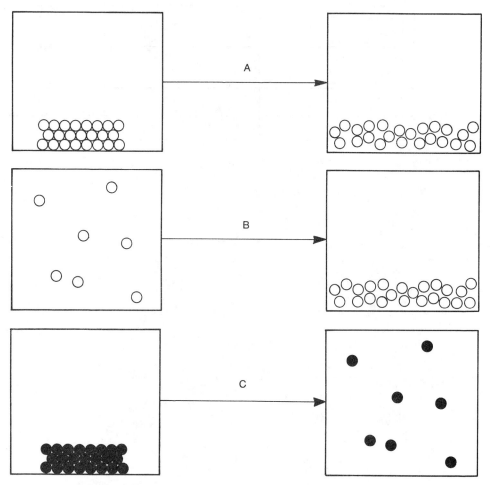

Which process, A, B or C,

a)   represents condensation?

b)   represents sublimation?

c)   involves the largest decrease in density?

d)   is the reverse of freezing?

2 Copy and complete the diagram below by adding the *reverse process* for each of those labelled.

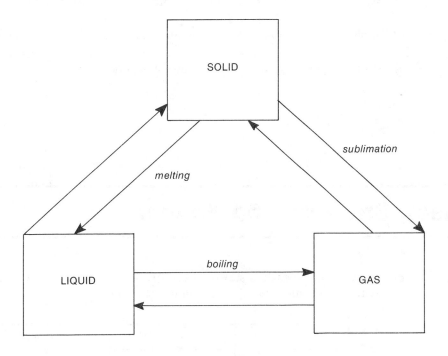

3 A substance melts at 92 °C and boils at 190 °C. The arrangement of particles in the substance at 50 °C and 250 °C are shown below.

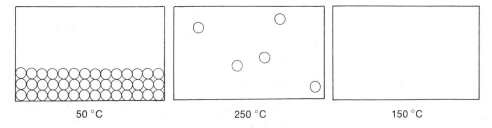

50 °C   250 °C   150 °C

a) Copy the diagrams, with labels, and draw in the arrangement of particles you would expect at 150°C.

b) At which of the three temperatures is the motion of the particles limited to vibration?

c) When the temperature of 10 g of the substance changes from 50°C to 60 °C, say whether each of the following quantities increases, decreases or stays the same. Give your reasons.

    i) the number of particles present

    ii) the average energy of the particles

    iii) the density of the substance.

4 Explain the following:

   a) When surgical spirit evaporates on your skin the area becomes cold.

   b) A burn from steam at 100 °C is worse than a burn from water at 100 °C.

   c) Panting helps dogs to cool down in hot weather.

Heat, Pressure and Volume

1 a) Use the data on the ten substances below to produce a table, which shows the state of each substance at room temperature (25 °C).

Substance	Melting point (°C)	Boiling point (°C)
Selenium	217	685
Anisole	−38	154
Beryllium	1280	2477
Bromine	−7	59
Propane	−188	−42
Benzamide	132	290
Cobalt	1492	2900
Radon	−71	−62
Anthracene	216	340
Propyne	−103	−23

Solids	Liquids	Gases

   b) List the substances in order of increasing boiling point.

   c) Which substance is a liquid over the smallest range of temperature?

   d) Which of the substances is/are gaseous at −50 °C?

   e) Which substance has the lowest freezing point?

   f) Which substance is a liquid at 2500 °C?

2 The diagram shows an alcohol thermometer, which uses an ethanol–dye mixture to indicate the temperature. Data on ethanol (and mercury, another liquid commonly used in thermometers) is given in the table.

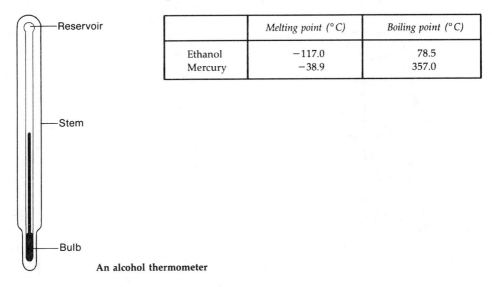

	Melting point (°C)	Boiling point (°C)
Ethanol	−117.0	78.5
Mercury	−38.9	357.0

An alcohol thermometer

a) i) Why does the bulb of the thermometer have thick glass at the base but thin glass around the sides?

   ii) Why is there a reservoir at the top of the stem?

b) Copy and complete the following table by listing one advantage and one disadvantage of each liquid for use in a thermometer.

	Advantage	Disadvantage
Ethanol		
Mercury		

c) The liquid in the alcohol thermometer freezes at −118.5 °C. Comment on this in view of the melting point of ethanol given.

3 The boiling point of a liquid increases as the external pressure increases. Use this information to explain the following observations.

a) If a cup of water is placed in an air-tight container and the air is removed using a vacuum pump, the water will boil without being heated.

b) Food cooks more quickly in a pressure cooker.

c) The accurately measured boiling point of a sample of pure water may change from one day to the next if there is an accompanying change in the weather.

d) It is dangerous to remove the radiator cap when a car's water cooling system is overheating.

4   Three rigid, hollow metal containers have tubes connected to beakers of water as shown in the diagram. All three contain air and are identical except for their internal conditions.

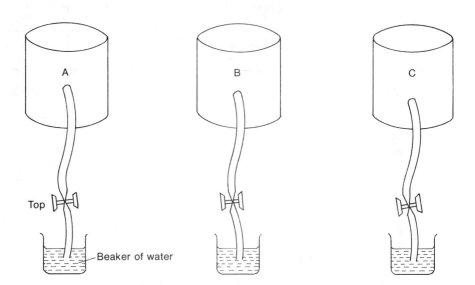

When the taps are opened, the following results are noted:

Container	Observations
A	The water level in the beaker drops
B	Nothing happens
C	Bubbles appear at the end of the tube

What can you deduce from these observations about the conditions inside each container before the taps were opened?

5 a) A partly inflated balloon is placed inside a glass container, which is then evacuated. As the air is pumped out of the container what will happen to

   i)   the number of molecules in the balloon?

   ii) the volume of the balloon?

   b) Explain why weather balloons, designed to fly at high altitude, are only partly inflated at launch.

6 a) A sample of gas at 1 atmosphere pressure is contained in a 100 cm^3 cylinder. If the piston is moved half way down the cylinder and no change in temperature occurs, what is the new value of

  i) the volume occupied by the gas

  ii) the pressure exerted by the gas?

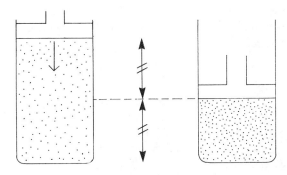

  b) In another experiment, the piston is moved down slowly so that the volume occupied by the gas is halved while the temperature remains constant. As a result of this, what has happened to

  i) the number of molecules in the cylinder?

  ii) the density of the gas?

  iii) the number of collisions per second by molecules on the piston?

7 The diagram below shows what happens inside a petrol engine cylinder.

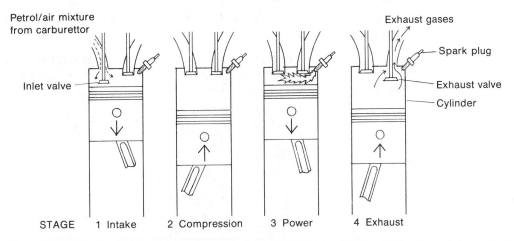

STAGE   1 Intake   2 Compression   3 Power   4 Exhaust

Petrol vapour and air are drawn in to the cylinder. The mixture is squeezed together and then exploded by a spark. The explosion pushes down the piston and this gives the engine power.

During which stage or stages does

a) the pressure and temperature in the cylinder increase.

b) the pressure and temperature in the cylinder increase without any chemical change.

c) the mean density of the gases in the cylinder increase.

d) the number of molecules in the cylinder increase.

8 The apparatus shown below is used to find the change in volume of a fixed mass of gas when the pressure is increased. The experiment is carried out at constant temperature.

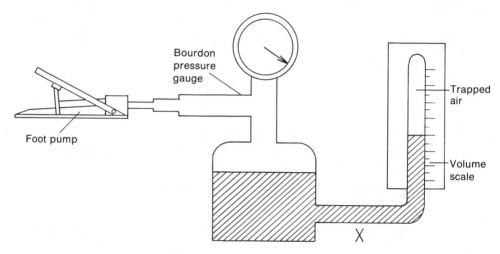

a) i) Write down a short description of what you would do, and what readings you would take, when carrying out this experiment.

  ii) What precaution would you include to allow the air to remain at its original temperature?

b) The graph below was produced using results from such an experiment. Use the graph to predict what will happen to the volume of a sample of gas when the pressure is doubled at constant temperature.

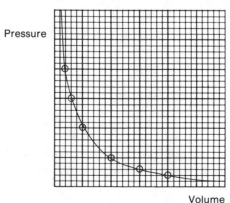

c) If a bubble of air was trapped in the apparatus at point X, what effect (if any) would this have on the results of the experiment?

9 The apparatus below is used to measure the pressure of a gas, at constant volume, as the temperature increases.

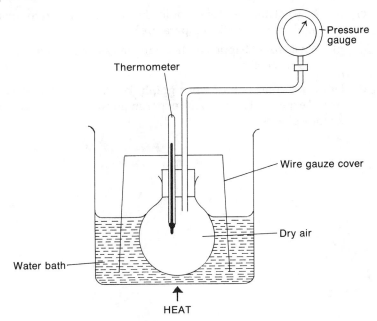

a) Why is a round-bottom flask preferred, and why is a cover needed?

b) What would happen to

   i)   the mass of gas in the flask?

   ii) the pressure of the gas

   as the temperature increases?

c) If the experiment is carried out at an external pressure of 1 atmosphere, what is the maximum temperature reached by the gas in the experiment?

d) Sketch the graph of pressure against temperature which you would obtain from such an experiment.

e) Explain in terms of the kinetic theory why the pressure of a gas changes as the temperature increases.

10 The volume of a sample of dry nitrogen was measured as its temperature changed. The pressure was maintained at 1 atmosphere throughout the experiment. The results obtained are shown in the table below:

Temperature (°C)	20	50	100	150	200	250
Volume (cm³)	48.1	53.0	61.2	69.4	77.6	85.8

a) Plot a graph of volume (y-axis) against temperature (x-axis). The x-axis scale should begin at -300 °C and extend to $+300$ °C with 50 °C per division. Draw the best-fit straight line through the points, and label it 'line A'.

b) Use your graph to estimate the volume of the nitrogen at $-100\,°C$ and 1 atmosphere.

c) i)   At what temperature would the sample have zero volume? What is the significance of this temperature?

ii) What would happen to the nitrogen gas on cooling before this temperature was reached?

d) Draw a second line on your graph, labelled 'line B', which shows what you would expect to happen if the experiment was repeated at a constant pressure of 2 atmospheres.

3 ATOMS

The Nucleus

1 a) Copy the following diagram of a helium atom and replace the letters A to D with labels from the following list:

nucleus   proton   neutron   electron

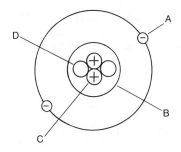

b) What is the total charge of

   i)   the nucleus

   ii)   the whole atom?

c) Copy and complete the sentence below to compare the masses of protons, neutrons and electrons.

   _____ and _____ are roughly _____ in mass, each being about 1800 times _____ than an _____.

2 Copy the following terms, and write a short definition underneath each:

a)   atomic number

b)   mass number

c)   isotope

3 A lithium atom can be described as $^{7}_{3}$Li. What is

a)   the atomic number

b)   the mass number

of lithium?

4 Details of the composition of five particles are given in the table.

Particle	Number of protons	Number of neutrons	Number of electrons
A	6	8	8
B	8	8	6
C	6	6	8
D	8	6	6
E	6	8	6

a) Which of the particles is a neutral atom?

b) Which particles are positive ions?

c) Which particles are ions carrying a charge of −2?

d) Which particle has the greatest mass?

e) Which particle is an isotope of E?

5 a) What are **isotopes** of an element?

b) The diagram below shows an atom of the most common isotope of oxygen, $^{16}_{8}$O.

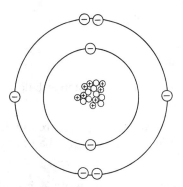

Two other isotopes of oxygen exist, $^{17}_{8}$O and $^{18}_{8}$O. Draw similar diagrams to show the atomic structure of these two isotopes

c) Copy and complete the passage below choosing the words from this list to fill in the blanks (each word may be used more than once):

unstable   **radioactive**   **rays**   **particles**   **nucleus**   **isotope**

All elements can have more than one _____. Many of them are _____. The _____ undergoes a change. When this happens α _____, β _____ or γ _____ may be emitted from the _____. This is called _____ decay.

Types of Decay

1 Copy and complete the following table, which concerns alpha, beta and gamma radiations.

Radiation type	Mass	Charge	Identity
Alpha particle			Helium nucleus
Beta particle	$\frac{1}{1800}$ units		
Gamma ray		Uncharged	

2 Which of the three common types of radiation

a) consists of positively charged particles

b) causes the most ionisation in air

c) is repelled by a positively charged plate

d) is not affected by a magnetic field

e) is absorbed by thin paper or skin

f) is only absorbed by thick lead or concrete

g) is absorbed by 3 mm of aluminium

h) can be detected by a gold leaf electroscope

i) cause blackening of a photographic film

j) can be detected using a Geiger–Muller tube?

3 a) Write down the following particle symbols and give the common name for each.

i) ^1_1H

ii) $^{\ 0}_{-1}\beta$

iii) ^2_1H

iv) ^1_0N

v) ^4_2He

b) Draw diagrams which show the structure of particles iii) and v).

4 a) Explain what is meant by the **half-life** of a radioactive isotope.

b) A sample of iodine-128 was monitored in an experiment and the following results obtained:

Time elapsed (minutes)	Count rate (counts/minute)
17	7080
29	5192
50	2816
60	2198
76	1364
105	662

The background count in the laboratory during the experiment was 80 counts/minute.

  i) Explain what the 'background count' is, and list two contributions to it.

  ii) Plot a graph of corrected count against time and use it to find the half-life of iodine-128.

5 The isotope $^{14}_{6}C$ has a half-life of 5600 years.

a) How many

  i) protons

  ii) neutrons are there in a nucleus of carbon-14?

b) After how long would a sample of carbon-14 decay to $\frac{1}{32}$ of the original count-rate?

c) Suggest why carbon-14 has been particularly useful in biochemical research.

d) Describe experiments using carbon-14 which show that

  i) the carbon dioxide breathed out by a small mammal comes from glucose eaten.

  ii) carbon dioxide is absorbed by a leaf during photosynthesis.

  iii) sugars made in leaves during photosynthesis are transported to other parts of the plant in the phloem.

6 a) Radon has a half-life of four days. How long will it take for $\frac{7}{8}$ of a sample of radon to decay?

b) Radium has a half-life of 1622 years. How long will it take for a 1.6 g sample of radium to decay until only 0.1 g remains?

7 Copy and complete the following nuclear reactions.

a) $^{24}_{12}Mg + ^{1}_{0}n \longrightarrow ^{24}_{11}Na + \boxed{}$

b) $^{24}_{11}Na \longrightarrow \boxed{} Mg + ^{0}_{-1}\beta$

c) $^{3}_{1}H \longrightarrow ^{3}_{2}He + \boxed{}$

d) $^{236}_{92}U \longrightarrow ^{144}_{56}Ba + ^{1}_{0}n + \boxed{} Kr$

e) $^{7}_{3}Li + ^{1}_{1}H \longrightarrow ^{4}_{2}He + \boxed{}$

8 Science makes use of models to help us to understand ideas which are not part of our everyday experience. Two models of the atom are shown below.

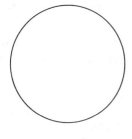

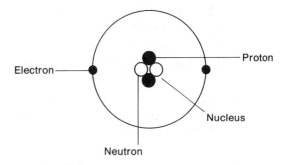

Model 1

spherical, electrically neutral, no internal structure

Model 2

spherical, with a small positively charged nucleus surrounded by negative electrons

How successful is each of the models in explaining the following? Explain your answer.

a) diffusion

b) a chemical reaction

c) radioactivity

Applications

1   A small domestic fire alarm contains a sample of radioactive Americium placed close
to two charged plates. Smoke particles from a fire cause a drop in the small current
flowing between the plates, triggering the alarm.

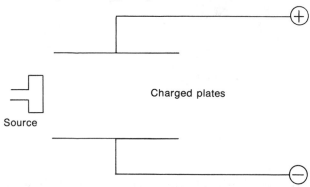

a)   What effect, due to the Americium, causes a small current to flow between the
plates?

b)   Explain how the presence of smoke particles causes the drop in current which
triggers the alarm.

c)   The operating instructions state that the unit should be wiped and vacuum
cleaned carefully at least every six months. Suggest a reason for this.

2   Plastic sheet can be made by an extrusion process known as calendering. The
thickness of the sheet, which must not vary too much, can be monitored using a
radioactive source and detector as shown in the diagram:

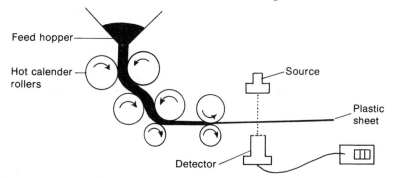

a)   Which type of source, alpha, beta or gamma, would *not* be suitable for this
application? Explain your choice.

b)   What is the name of the type of detector commonly used to detect radioactivity?

c)   Explain how the source and detector can be used to monitor the thickness of the
sheet.

3 Some forms of cancer can be treated using radiotherapy. Before treatment, the position of a tumour in the body is found. Two beams of radiation can then be directed at the tumour, each of just over one-half of the intensity needed to destroy tissue.

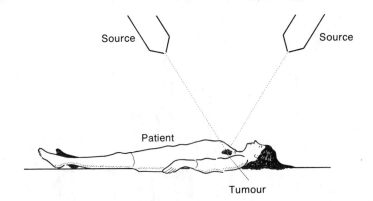

a) Explain why this procedure is of greater benefit to the patient than using a single (more powerful) beam.

b) Explain how rotating a single powerful source (or the patient) about an axis through the tumour is an equally useful method.

c) Why are the radioactive isotopes used in *diagnosis* almost always gamma sources?

4 Describe the use of radioactive isotopes in the following situations. In each case say

i) whether a suitable isotope should have a half-life measured in seconds, hours, days or years

ii) whether the type of source (α, β or γ) is important.

a) tracing leaks in underground pipes

b) revealing blockages in the human circulatory system

c) testing the thickness of cardboard during manufacture.

5 1. One uranium-235 nucleus can release 3×10^{-11} J.

2. 1 kg of uranium-235 contains 3×10^{24} atoms.

3. 1 kg of coal can produce 3×10^{10} J on combustion.

Use the information provided to calculate the mass of coal needed to produce the same amount of energy as 1 g of uranium-235.

6 Trace the diagram of a nuclear reactor and replace the letters A–F with labels from the following list:

uranium oxide fuel rods   **boron control rods**   **graphite moderator**

concrete pressure vessel   **steel lining**   **circulating gas**

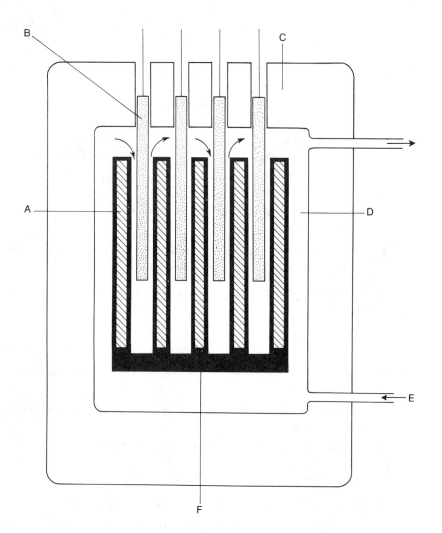

Theme 2

Forces

1 TYPES AND SIZE OF FORCE

Forces and their Effects

1   a)   Choose all the words from the list below which could correctly complete this
             sentence:

   Forces can change the _____ of an object.

   colour   direction of movement   mass   shape   size   speed

   b)   Copy and complete this statement of Newton's first law of motion:

   A body stays at _____ or moves at a constant _____ in a _____
   line unless it is acted upon by an external _____.

   c)   Copy and complete these sentences:

   Forces are measured in units called _____.

   The pull of the Earth or the force of gravity on a body is called its _____
   and is measured in _____.

   The pull of the Earth on a mass of 1 kg is approximately _____.

   d)   Which force is responsible for the following effects?
   i)   A book sliding across a desk slows down and stops.
   ii) A book falls to the ground when dropped.
   iii) The Moon remains in orbit around the Earth.
   iv) A polystyrene block rises to the water's surface when released from the
        bottom of a swimming pool.

2   a)   i)   List *four* ways in which friction is a nuisance.
             ii) List *four* ways in which friction is useful.

   b)   Explain
   i)   how aborigines can light fires by rubbing two sticks together.
   ii) why spacecraft can get very hot when they re-enter the Earth's atmosphere.

   c)   i)   What single word would describe the *shape* of a rocket, a high speed train,
             a fish, and a cheetah at full speed?
             ii) What is the advantage of being such a shape?

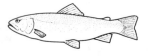

3 a) List *five* ways of reducing friction.

b) You are walking to school one day and the force of friction suddenly disappears. Write an account of what might happen.

4 The drawing shows a ball being kicked.

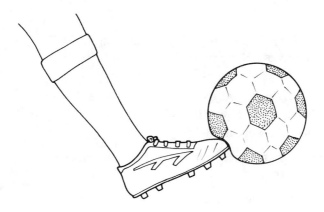

a) Draw an arrow on the drawing to show the direction of the force acting on the ball due to

i) the kick

ii) gravity.

b) How can you tell from the ball in the drawing that there is a force on it?

c) What shape will the ball be when it is moving through the air?

d) Apart from gravity, which other force acts on the ball in the air?

5

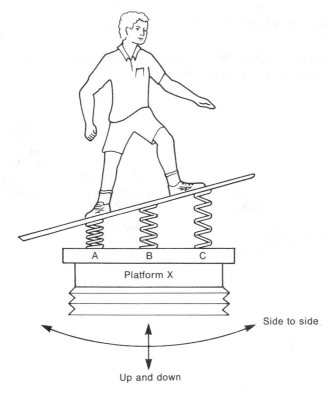

Natural length of spring

Platform X

Side to side

Up and down

A pupil is riding on a surfing simulator at a fairground. The motor moves a platform X from side to side, and up and down. The 3 springs A, B and C are identical.

a) i) Which spring, A, B or C, has the greatest force acting on it as shown in the diagram?

    ii) How did you decide?

b) Write down the correct reading on the newtonmeter shown here.

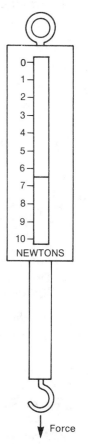

NEWTONS

Force

6 When a 20 g mass is suspended from a spring, the extension produced in the spring is 10 cm.

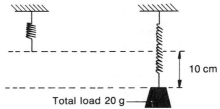

Total load 20 g

10 cm

What extension would you expect in each of the identical springs, in the following experiments?

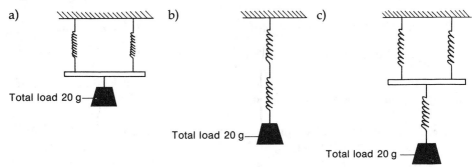

a)   b)   c)

Total load 20 g

Total load 20 g

Total load 20 g

7

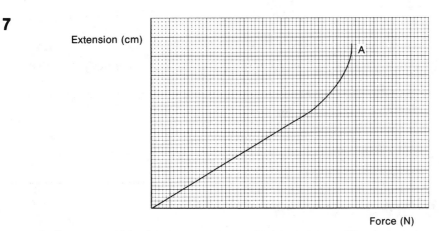

Extension (cm)

A

Force (N)

The graph shows how the extension produced in a spring varies as the force applied to the spring increases.

a)   State Hooke's law. When does it apply?

b)   Copy the graph and label the following:
   i) the elastic limit
   ii) the region where Hooke's law is obeyed

c)   i) Label a point X on the curve where plastic deformation has occurred.
   ii) What would you see happening to the spring if the magnitude of the applied force was increased beyond point A?

8   The graphs below show how two materials behave when stretched.

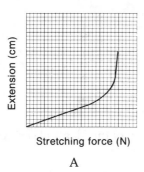

A

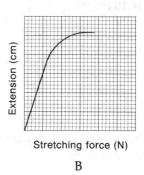

B

a)   Describe the difference in the way the two materials behave.

b)   Which one is steel and which one is rubber?

c)   Why is it important for an engineer involved in designing a bridge to know how metals behave under tension?

9   Copy and complete these sentences about balanced and unbalanced forces, choosing words from this list to fill in the blanks.

acceleration   balanced   constant   equilibrium   unbalanced

a)   If the forces acting on a body are _____, the body will be stationary or move at a _____ speed in a straight line.

b)   If the forces acting on a body are _____, the body will accelerate.

c)   A body is said to be in _____ under the action of several forces when it has an _____ of zero.

Combining Forces

1   a)   Copy and complete the sentences below using the words **size** or **direction** to fill in the blanks.
        i) Force is a vector quantity because both _____ and _____ are important.
        ii) Scalar quantities have only _____ and no _____.

    b)   Give *two* other examples of vector quantities.

    c)   Give *three* examples of scalar quantities.

2 The diagrams below show the size and direction of a number of forces applied to a wooden block. Draw a similar diagram for each example, which shows the magnitude (size) and direction of the single resultant (overall) force. Show how you arrived at your answer for parts c) to f).

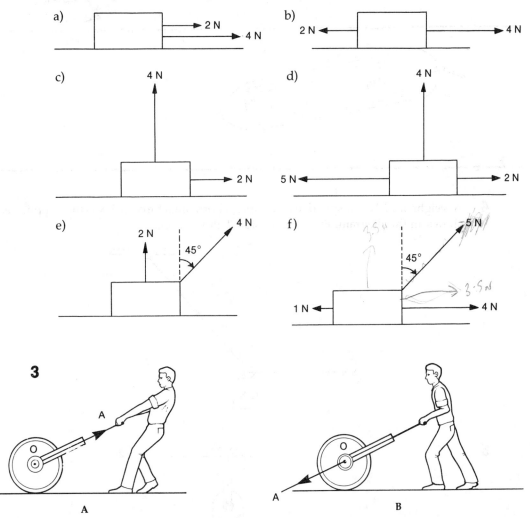

3

a) The diagram A shows a man pulling a garden roller with a force represented by the line OA. On a similar diagram (you need not draw the man), show the horizontal and the vertical components of the force.

b) The diagram B shows a man pushing a garden roller with a force represented by the line OA. On a similar diagram show the horizontal and vertical components of the force.

c) The man wants to move his garden roller to a different part of his garden across a wet muddy lawn. Should he pull or push the roller? Explain your answer.

d) On another occasion he wants to roll his dry lawn. Should he pull or push this time? Explain your answer.

e) The diagram below shows a barge being towed from the canal bank. To avoid hitting the bank, the barge must steer towards the centre of the river. Copy the diagram and draw in the forces acting, to explain why this is so.

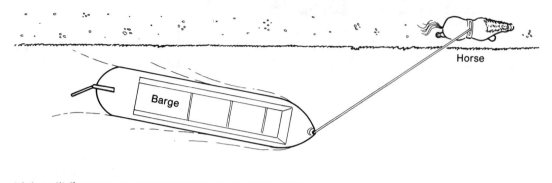

4 A weight of 12 N is suspended by a rope. A horizontal force of 5 N is then applied as shown in the diagram. Find the tension T in the rope.

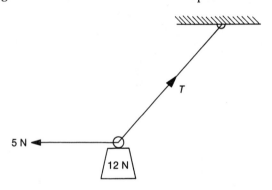

5

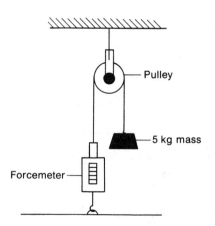

A 5 kg mass is suspended over a pulley. The rope is connected to a forcemeter which has its hook anchored to the floor. What is the reading on the forcemeter? ($g = 10$ N/kg)

Forces in Balance

1 The following objects are in equilibrium. Copy (or trace) each diagram and draw in the missing force or forces, paying particular attention to their direction of action. Label all the forces, choosing your answer from the following list. (Each one may be used more than once if necessary.)

reaction   **weight**   **tension**   **drag**   **friction**

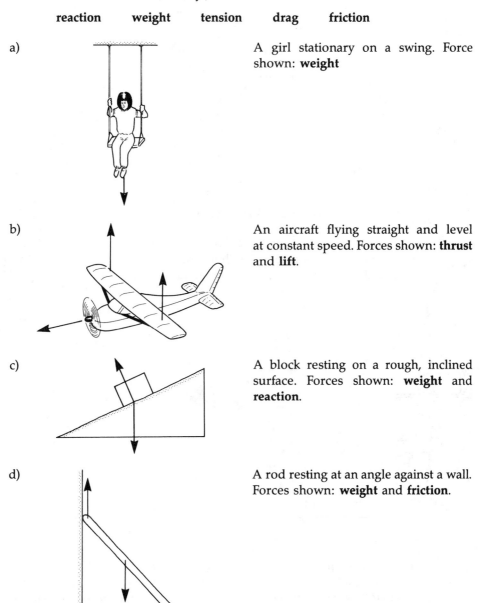

a)   A girl stationary on a swing. Force shown: **weight**

b)   An aircraft flying straight and level at constant speed. Forces shown: **thrust** and **lift**.

c)   A block resting on a rough, inclined surface. Forces shown: **weight** and **reaction**.

d)   A rod resting at an angle against a wall. Forces shown: **weight** and **friction**.

2 A 'manoeuvring unit' (MU) designed to allow astronauts to travel from the Space
Shuttle on short journeys into space is shown in the diagram. It is fitted with a compressed gas cylinder and six jets which can fire jets of gas in the directions indicated.
By activating certain jets the astronaut is able to move in any desired direction. The
force exerted by each jet acts through the centre of mass of the astronaut-chair unit,
and the jets are arranged in opposing pairs.

Chair-shaped
manoeuvering unit
(MU) showing the
siz jets A–F

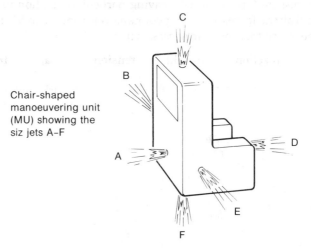

Chair-shaped manoeuvring unit (MU) showing the six jets A–F.

On one particular mission to retrieve a damaged satellite in orbit (mass 8 000 kg)
an astronaut emerges from the Shuttle and moves towards the satellite along the
route indicated. (The diagram is not to scale.)

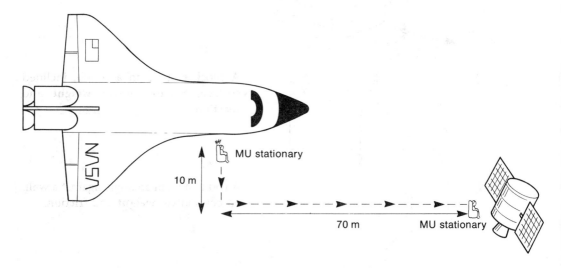

a) To move off as shown, the astronaut fires a short burst of gas from jet C. Write
down the complete sequence of jets which must be fired to enable the astronaut
to follow the route indicated. Assume that each jet exerts the same force for the
same time.

b)   What advantage is there in arranging the jets of the MU

   i) in opposing pairs?

   ii) so that all exert a force through the centre of mass of the system?

c)   Is it possible for the astronaut to make the MU rotate while strapped in and well away from other objects? Explain your answer.

d)   While trying to turn a screw on one of the satellite panels, the astronaut and MU begin to rotate. Explain how this occurs.

3   The bottle in the diagram is in equilibrium in three positions A, B and C.

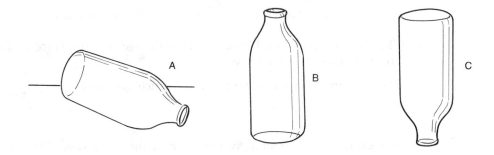

a)   In which position is the bottle in

   i) stable equilibrium?

   ii) unstable equilibrium?

   iii) neutral equilibrium?

   Explain your choices.

b)   Copy this sentence choosing only the correct alternative from inside the brackets.

   To be more stable an object should have a (high/low) centre of mass and a (narrow/broad) base.

c)   Why does the giraffe shown here splay out its front legs as it takes a drink?

Moments

1   When Margaret and Richard sit on the see-saw it does not balance:

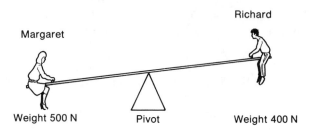

Margaret

Richard

Weight 500 N   Pivot   Weight 400 N

a)   What force is needed on Richard's end of the see-saw to balance it? Give the direction and size of the force.

b)   Who must move closer to the pivot to balance the see-saw?

2   The **moment** of a force about a pivot is given by the expression

moment = magnitude of force × perpendicular distance from pivot

A moment has a turning effect on objects.

a)   i) Why is it very difficult to close a door by pushing close to the hinges, yet very easy when the same force is applied near the handle?

ii) Why is it easier to rotate a nut using a spanner with a long handle?

b)   Where should a downward force of 200 N be applied to balance the beam shown below?

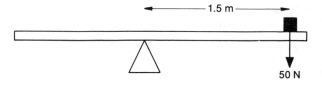

1.5 m

50 N

3 Describe how you would use the following apparatus to find the mass of a potato, estimated to be 200 g.

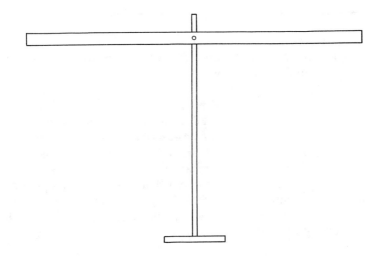

metre rule balanced on a nail through its mid-point

string, as required

one 150 g mass, with a hole at its centre

one potato

4 The object drawn below has the centre of mass marked by a small circle. Describe the effect of the force or forces acting on the object in each situation. All forces shown have the same magnitude (size).

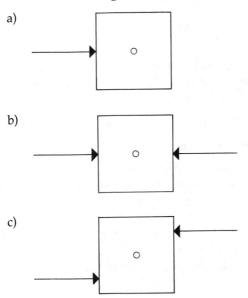

a)

b)

c)

2 MASS AND WEIGHT

1 Copy and complete the following paragraph which compares **mass** and **weight** using the words in the list below.

> **matter**   **mass**   **force**   **velocity**   **60**   **100**

_____ is measured in kilograms, and represents the amount of _____ present in an object. It can also be described as the resistance of an object to changes in _____. If you took an object of mass 60 kg (as measured on Earth) to the Moon, it would have a mass of _____ kg. Weight is an example of a _____. On Earth, a person with a mass of 60 kg is pulled towards the centre of the Earth with a force of 600 N. On the Moon, the same person would weigh _____ N, because the acceleration due to gravity there is approximately one-sixth of that on Earth.

2 Given an inertia balance (wig-wag) and a timer, together with three rods each of mass 0.10 kg, explain how you would find the mass of another rod, thought to be about 0.15 kg.

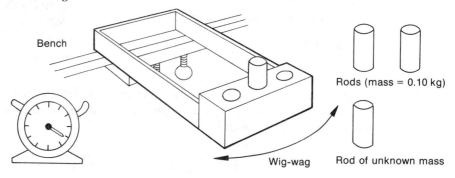

3 Two identical space vehicles (each of mass 500 kg) are at rest, one on the surface of the Moon and the other on Mercury. (Gravitational field strengths: Moon 1.6 N/kg, Mercury 3.6 N/kg.)

a) What would be the mass of each vehicle as measured at each site?

b) What would the weight of each vehicle be?

c) Richard believes that the force needed to give the vehicle a horizontal acceleration of 1 m/s^2 is greater on Mercury than on the Moon. David thinks that the force required would be the same in each case. Who is correct, and why?

4 Two gas cylinders have been found. One is known to contain a poisonous gas under pressure, the other a partial vacuum, but they are identical in all other respects. In principle, would it be possible to identify the poison gas cylinder by weighing them?

Explain your answer.

3 PRESSURE

1 Copy and complete this formula:

$$\text{force} = \underline{\hspace{3cm}} \times \text{area}$$
$$\text{(N)} \qquad\qquad\qquad \text{(m}^2\text{)}$$

(You may need to use this formula in the questions which follow.)

2 A rectangular block has dimensions $10 \times 20 \times 40$ cm. It is made from material with density 2200 kg/m^3.

a) What is the volume of the block in m^3?

b) What is the mass of the block?

c) What is the weight of the block? ($g = 10 \text{ N/kg}$)

d) What pressure does the block exert when standing on its smallest face?

e) Would the block float or sink in water (density 1000 kg/m^3)? Explain your answer.

(Additional formula: mass $=$ volume $\times$ density.)

3 Calculate the pressure in Pa ($1 \text{ Pa} = 1 \text{ N/m}^2$) exerted in the following situations:

a) a circus stilt-walker, total weight 1000 N, balancing on one stilt (area 0.001 m^2).

b) a circus elephant, weight 50 000 N, balancing on its hind legs (total surface area in contact with the ground 0.10 m^2).

4 A hydraulic jack is shown below.

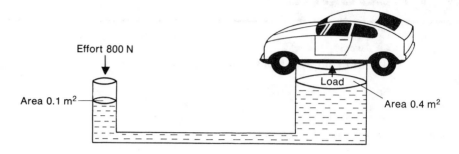

a) What pressure does the effort exert?

b) What force is transmitted to the load?

c) What is the mechanical advantage of the jack?

$$\left(\text{Additional formula: mechanical advantage} = \frac{\text{load}}{\text{effort}}. \right)$$

5 Paving stones are made of a composite material. They often crack with no visible sign that this is about to happen, as pressure on a slab from above causes a crack to appear on the underside.

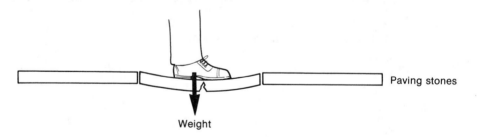

a) i) What is a composite material?

   ii) Which composite is used to make paving stones?

b) Using the formula

$$\text{pressure} = \frac{\text{force}}{\text{area}}$$

calculate the pressure exerted when a man (weight 800 N) stands on a paving stone (total area of feet in contact with the stone 0.02 m²).

c) i) Which surface of the paving stone is under compression?

   ii) Which surface of the paving stone is under tension?

   iii) Is the material stronger in compression or tension? Explain your answer.

6

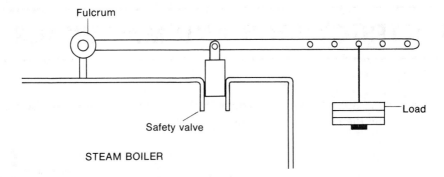

The diagram shows a steam boiler safety valve, which is designed to operate when the pressure in the boiler reaches 200 kPa.

a) Write down the pressure, in N/m², at which the valve operates.

b) In the arrangement shown, the downward force on the valve due to the load is 500 N. Calculate the area of the hole in which the valve is seated.

c) Would the valve operating pressure increase or decrease if the load was moved closer to the fulcrum? Explain your choice.

7 A length of rubber tubing is filled with water and lowered into a water tank as shown in the diagram.

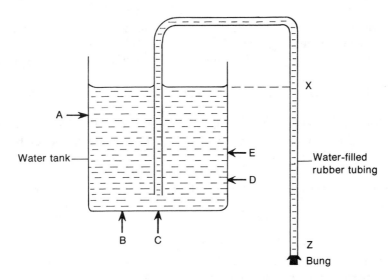

a) At which two of the positions A–E is the pressure on the inside wall of the tank the same?

b) i) What is the pressure inside the tubing at X?

   ii) Is the pressure at Z greater or less than that of X? Explain your answer.

c) Describe fully what happens when the bung at Z is removed. Give reasons for your answer.

4 STRUCTURES AND MATERIALS

1 Two similar metal bars, made of steel and aluminium, are tested by hanging weights from their mid-points as shown in the diagram.

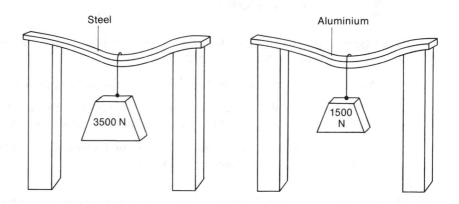

Steel		**Aluminium**	
Mass	7.9 kg	Mass	2.7 kg
Melting point	1535 °C	Melting point	650 °C
Cost	£35/tonne	Cost	£950/tonne

The bars are shown with just enough weight to cause bending.

a) The metal used to make bridges needs to be able to bend slightly without breaking. Give *two* reasons why steel would be better than aluminium for making bridges.

b) Why would aluminium be better than steel to use in making a space station?

2 In a structure, a component under **tension** is called a **tie**, while a component under **compression** is called a **strut**.

Copy the diagrams of structures below and for each one say whether it shows compression or tension, and whether it is a strut or a tie. (The arrows represent forces.)

a)

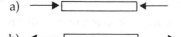

b)

3 For each structure a) to d), state whether the labelled components (A, B and C) are struts or ties. See the previous question for definitions of struts and ties.

a)

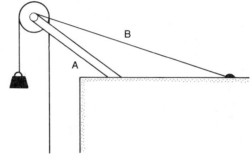

b)

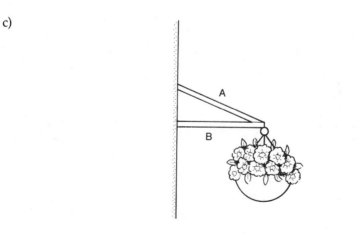

c)

d)

4 a) The ties in the Forth Rail Bridge are conventional lattice girders, while the struts are made from tubular steel components, up to 3.6 m in diameter.

    i) What is the advantage of using tubular steel components compared with solid steel of the same diameter?

    ii) What is the advantage of using tubular components over those made from the same amount of material in solid form?

  b) List two advantages of hollow bones to birds.

Theme 3

Motion

1 MOVING ON

Velocity

1 Prakesh decides to go to Amrit's home to collect some heavy books. The graph shows how his distance from home (in metres) changes with time (in minutes):

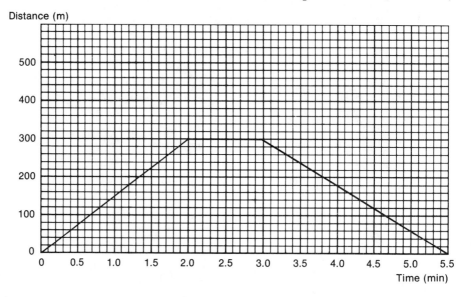

a) How long did it take Prakesh to reach Amrit's home?

b) How far away is Amrit's house?

c) What was Prakesh's average speed on the outward journey in m/s?

d) How long did Prakesh stay at Amrit's house?

2 a) Copy and complete this formula.

$$\text{average speed} = \frac{\underline{\hspace{2cm}} \text{ travelled}}{\underline{\hspace{2cm}} \text{ taken}}$$

b) Calculate the average speed of the following:
   i) a runner who travels 100 m in 10 s
   ii) a cyclist who travels 48 km in 3 hours
   iii) a car which travels 240 km in 3 hours
   iv) a rocket which travels 400 000 km in 80 hours

3 a) Copy and complete the formula

distance travelled = _____ × time taken

b) The nearest star to the Sun (and Earth), Proxima Centauri, is approximately 4 light years from Earth. 1 light year may be taken to be 9 million million km (9×10^{12} km). How long would it take a space ship, travelling at 60 000 kilometres per hour, to reach Proxima Centauri?

4 Copy and complete the passage below which is about speed and velocity. Choose words from this list to fill in the blanks:

> constant direction gradient scalar speed straight
> time vector

The velocity of an object is an indication of both the speed and the _____ in which it is moving. Velocity is a _____ quantity, whilst speed is a _____ quantity. Plotting a graph of the distance travelled against _____ taken allows us to find the _____ of an object. If the body is travelling at a _____ speed the graph will be a _____ line and the speed will be the _____ of that line.

5 The overall stopping distances for a car travelling at various speeds are listed in the table.

Car speed (m.p.h.)	Thinking distance (feet)	Braking distance (feet)	Overall stopping distance (feet)
30	30	45	75
40	40	80	120
50	50	125	175
60	60	180	240
70	70	245	315

a) i) What is the 'thinking distance'?

   ii) Using the pattern in the thinking distances, write down the thinking distance in feet when travelling at 100 m.p.h.

b) i) What is the pattern relating the braking distance (in feet) to the speed of the car (in m.p.h.)?

   ii) Use your answer to b) i) to calculate the braking distance for a car travelling at 100 m.p.h.

c) What is the overall stopping distance for a car travelling at 100 m.p.h.?

d) List three reasons why the actual stopping distance for a car travelling at 100 m.p.h. may not be the same as the value correctly calculated in part c).

6   A student set up the following experiment to measure the velocity of a trolley moving down a slope.

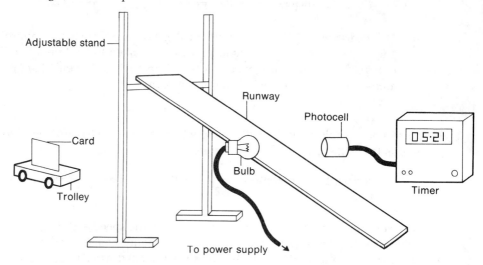

The card on the trolley blocks the light from the bulb as the trolley moves down the runway. The time taken for the card to pass in front of the photocell is recorded on the timer.

a)   i) If the trolley moves down the runway at constant velocity, what can you say about the forces acting on the trolley while it is moving?

ii) What information, other than the reading on the timer, is needed to calculate the velocity of the trolley?

b)   The angle of the slope is increased so that the trolley accelerates down the runway.

i) What forces are acting on the trolley in the direction of the slope? Comment on the relative size of these forces.

ii) Describe how you would modify the experiment in order to calculate the acceleration of the trolley. List any additional measurements you would need to take, and how you would calculate the acceleration of the trolley from your measurements.

Acceleration

1   Acceleration is given by the formula

$$\text{acceleration} = \frac{\text{change in velocity (m/s)}}{\text{time taken for change (s)}}$$

Copy the formula and add the units used to measure acceleration.

2 A new sports car undergoing trials accelerates to 30 m/s. After maintaining this speed for some time it decelerates to rest in two stages. This information is shown on the velocity–time graph.

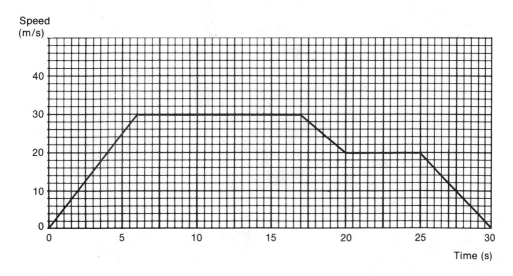

a) What was the acceleration of the car during the first six seconds?

b) i) For what length of time was the car travelling at 30 m/s?
   ii) What distance did it travel in that time?

c) Find the total distance travelled during the short trial by calculating the area under the graph.

d) Copy and complete the following:

If a graph is plotted of speed against time an object's _____ can be found by the _____ of the graph. The area under the graph gives the total _____ travelled.

3 a) Copy and complete this sentence.

To maintain circular motion, a force acting towards the _____ of the circle is needed, which is known as the centripetal force.

b) In each of the following situations, an object is in circular motion. Identify the centripetal force in each case.

   i)

   A boy whirling a conker on a string

ii)

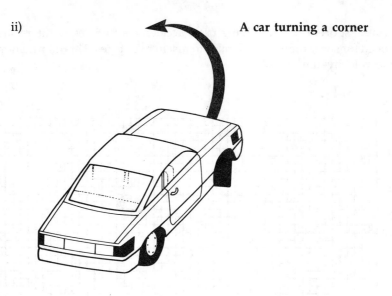

A car turning a corner

iii)

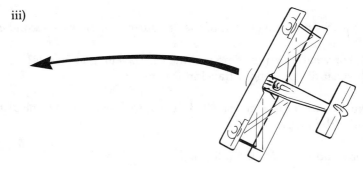

An aeroplane turning at constant height

iv)

The Moon orbiting the Earth

4 Calculate the acceleration of the following objects, stating the units clearly.

a) A sprinter accelerating from rest to a velocity of 5 m/s in 5 s.

b) A falling apple which hits the ground at 5 m/s after falling for 0.5 s.

c) A rocket which reaches a velocity of 150 km/h, 5 s after launch.

d) A train which decelerates uniformly from 120 km/h and stops after 1 min.

e) A car which crashes at 50 km/h and is brought to rest in 1 s.

(Formula: change in velocity $=$ acceleration $\times$ time taken.)

5 a) Copy and complete this formula. Include units inside the brackets.

force (_____) $=$ _____ (_____) $\times$ acceleration (_____)

b) Use the formula to calculate the acceleration of a lorry, mass 3000 kg, when acted on by a force of 2400 N.

c) What force is needed to decelerate the same lorry at 2.0 m/s²?

d) A second lorry accelerates at 0.5 m/s² when acted on by a force of 2200 N. What is its mass?

6 A car of mass 1200 kg, is travelling at a steady 30 m/s. The driver brakes and the car stops after 6 s.

a) Assuming that the deceleration is uniform, how fast is the car travelling 3 s after the brakes are applied?

b) Calculate the deceleration in m/s².

c) What braking force was applied?
(Formulae: change in velocity $=$ acceleration $\times$ time taken
force $=$ mass $\times$ acceleration.)

7 The diagram below shows a stone attached to a string held at O, and being swung round in a **vertical** circle (i.e. in a vertical plane).

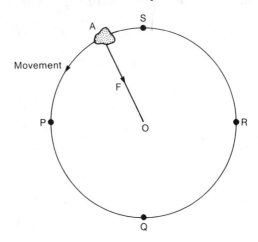

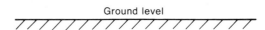
Ground level

a) A force, F, acting inwards on the stone at position A keeps the stone moving in a circle. What do we call force F?

b) What provides force F when the stone is at position P?

c) Draw on the diagram the **separate paths** that the stone will follow until it hits the ground if the string breaks at P, Q, R and S.

Momentum

1 The momentum, p, of an object is given by the expression

$$p = mv$$

where m is the mass of the object in kg and v is its velocity in m/s.

a) Which of the following units is momentum measured in?

   kg/m/s   **kg.m/s**   **kg/m.s**   **kg.m.s**

    b)   Calculate the momentum of the following objects:

        i) A ball, mass 100 g, travelling at 10 m/s.

        ii) An athlete, mass 60 kg, running at 8 m/s.

        iii) A car, mass 900 kg, moving at 30 m/s.

2 Two asteroids are on a collision course in deep space. One is approaching the other at a relative velocity of 4 km/s as shown.

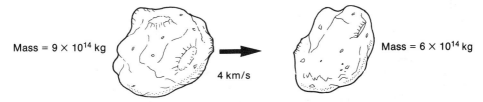

Mass = 9×10^{14} kg   4 km/s   Mass = 6×10^{14} kg

Assuming that the asteroids form a single larger body after collision, calculate:

a)   the mass of the body

b)   the velocity of the body

3 a)   A 500 g cannon fires a cannon ball (mass 20 kg) horizontally at 50 m/s. Calculate the velocity of recoil of the cannon.

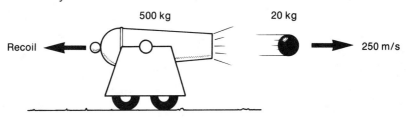

500 kg   20 kg

Recoil   250 m/s

    (Formula: momentum = mass × velocity.)

    b)   Ignoring effects due to air resistance, what is:

        i) the horizontal component of the velocity when the cannon ball hits the ground?

        ii) the shape of the curved path followed by the cannon ball?

4 After launch, a firework rocket reaches a height of 50 m. As it reaches its maximum height, it breaks into three fragments. Two of the fragments travel in directions X and Y. Which of the directions marked A, B and C must represent the direction of the third fragment? Explain your choice.

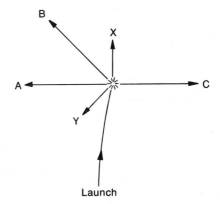

Theme 4

Energy Transfer

1 KINETIC AND POTENTIAL ENERGY

Situations and Calculations – Work and Power

1   Copy and complete the following table showing some energy conversions in a motor car.

Device	Conversion
Battery	_____ → electrical energy
Headlamps	electrical energy → _____
Horn	_____ → sound energy
Brakes	kinetic energy → _____
Engine	thermal energy → _____

2   Copy the statements below, choosing the correct words from this list to fill in the blanks.

> **newton   force   created   watt   power   work   metre**
> **conservation   destroyed   changed**

a)   Energy transferred is equal to the _____ done.

b)   One joule is the work done when a force of one _____ acts over a distance of one _____ (in the direction of the _____).

c)   Energy cannot be _____ or _____ but it can be _____ from one form to another. This is the principle of _____ of energy.

d)   _____ is the rate of doing work.

e)   A rate of doing work of one joule per second is equal to one _____.

3   Copy the formulae below and include the correct units chosen from the list:

> **watts   seconds   newtons   metres   joules**

a)   work done   =   force   × distance moved
     (_____)   (_____) (_____)

b)   power   = $\dfrac{\text{work done (_____)}}{\text{time taken (_____)}}$
     (_____)

4 a) A man of mass 80 kg climbs a flight of stairs to get from the ground floor to his second floor flat. Each step is 0.2 m high and there are 30 steps. How much work does he do against gravity?

b) If it takes him 10 s to run up the stairs, how much power does he develop?

c) What energy changes are involved in running up the stairs?

d) The next day he takes the lift instead of using the stairs. If the lift has a mass of 250 kg, how much work is done by the motor which drives the lift?

5 Below are some pairs of statements about kinetic and potential energy. Consider each pair and decide which one to put into which column in a table with the headings shown below. Copy and complete the table.

Gravitational potential energy	Kinetic energy

a) Energy that a body has because of its movement.
Energy that a body has because of its position.

b) A diver standing on the high board has it.
A fast moving racing car on a level track has it.

c) It increases as an object accelerates (horizontally).
It increases as an object is raised to a greater height (at a steady rate).

d) It is found using the formula: mass × g × height
(kg) (10 N/kg) (m)
It is found using the formula: 1/2 × mass × velocity squared
(kg) $(m/s)^2$

e) Is measured in joules.
Is also measured in joules.

6 The kinetic energy of an object of mass m (kg) moving with velocity v (m/s) is given by the formula

$$\text{kinetic energy} = \tfrac{1}{2}mv^2$$

Use this expression to calculate the kinetic energy (J) of the following objects.

a) A snowball, mass 0.1 kg, thrown at 12 m/s.

b) An athlete, mass 50 kg, running at a steady 8 m/s.

c) A bullet, mass 20 g, travelling at 500 m/s.

d) A proton, mass 1.7×10^{-27} kg travelling at 3.0×10^7 m/s.

e) An insect, mass 1.5 g, crawling at 0.02 m/s.

7   A pendulum bob is originally at rest at O, suspended from point X. It is raised to point A then released. It travels past O and reaches point C. Copy the diagram together with the following sentences, which you should complete by adding the appropriate word or words.

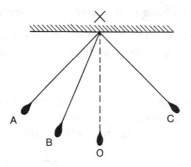

a)   At point A, the pendulum bob has _____ energy only.

b)   At point B the pendulum bob has both _____ and _____ energy.

c)   At point O, after being released, the pendulum bob has _____ energy only.

d)   The velocity of the bob is greatest at point _____.

e)   The acceleration of the bob is greatest at points _____ and _____.

8   a)   Copy and complete the following sentence by choosing the correct alternative inside each bracket.

The greater the (force/speed/time) of an object, the greater the (force/speed/time) needed to stop it in a given (force/speed/time).

b)   Study the table below, which gives the minimum stopping distance for a locomotive travelling at various speeds.

Speed (m/s)	Stopping distance (m)
10	40
20	160
30	360
40	640

i) Plot a graph of stopping distance against speed and use it to estimate the stopping distance when the locomotive is travelling at 25 m/s.

ii) Assuming that the locomotive decelerates uniformly, calculate the time taken to stop when travelling at 20 m/s using the formula

distance travelled = average speed × time

iii) What happens to the kinetic energy lost by the locomotive in slowing down?

iv) Would you expect these stopping distances to increase or decrease when the locomotive was pulling a number of carriages? Explain your answer.

v) Which of the formulae below relates the stopping distance to the speed of the locomotive? (s = stopping distance, v = speed)

1) $s = 0.5\,v$
2) $s^2 = 4\,v$
3) $s = 4\,v^2$
4) $s = 0.4\,v^2$
5) $2.5\,s = v^2$

Mechanisms and Machines

1 Rotary motion can be transferred using meshed gear wheels. In the example drawn below, the driver wheel (input) has 20 teeth, and the driven wheel (output) has 10 teeth.

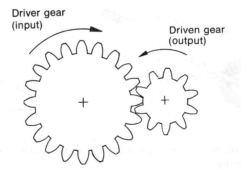

Driver gear
(input)

Driven gear
(output)

a) When the driver gear has completed one revolution, how many revolutions has the driven gear completed?

b) To enable the output rotation to be in the same direction as that of the input, a third 'idler' gear can be introduced between the two gear wheels.

i) Draw a diagram to show how this is achieved.

ii) Would the number of teeth on the idler gear make any difference to the relative rate of rotation of the input and output gear wheels?

2   Study the diagrams of the three classes of lever shown below, then decide to which class each of the levers a)–f) belongs.

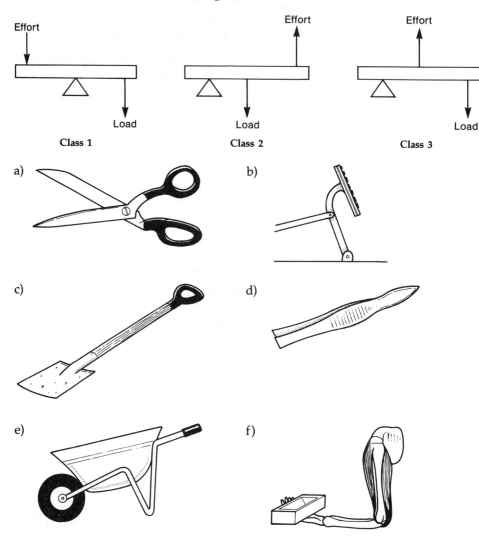

3   Copy the information below which is about **machines** using words from this list to fill in the blanks:

                effort   **energy**   **forces**   **load**

Machines help us to apply _____ more easily. A machine is a mechanism for transferring _____. The force applied to a machine is called the _____. Something called the _____ is moved by the machine. Ideally a large _____ is moved by a small _____.

4   Make a list of the levers you can find in your home. For each one say whether it is a *force multiplier* or a *distance multiplier*.

5 a) Copy and complete these formulae:

i) $\dfrac{\rule{3cm}{0.4pt}}{} = \dfrac{\text{load}}{\text{effort}}$

ii) velocity ratio (VR) $= \dfrac{\text{distance moved by} \rule{2cm}{0.4pt}}{\text{distance moved by} \rule{2cm}{0.4pt}}$

b)   i) A machine has a mechanical advantage of 10. What does this mean?

ii) A machine has a velocity ratio of 3. What does this mean?

iii) Write down *two* formulae which can be used to calculate the percentage efficiency of a machine.

d) A machine has an efficiency of 50%. What does this mean?

e) Explain why it is necessary to keep the moving parts of a machine well lubricated.

6

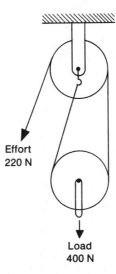

Effort
220 N

Load
400 N

The pulley system shown above is used to move a load of 400 N. The effort moves through a distance of 1.0 m while the load moves through a distance of 0.5 metres.

Calculate:

a) the mechanical advantage of the pulley

b) the velocity ratio of the pulley

c) the work done in lifting the load (Formula: work done = force × distance moved)

d) the work done by the effort

e) the efficiency of the pulley

7 Using a block and tackle, an engine is hoisted out of a car. The engine has a mass (*m*) of 400 kg and is raised to a height (*h*) of 1.5 metres.

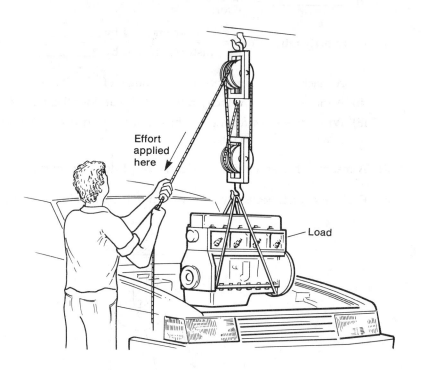

Effort applied here

Load

a) Use the expression

$$\text{work done} = m.g.h$$

to calculate the work done in raising the engine through 1.5 m against gravity. (*g* = 10 N/kg)

b) The mechanic operating the block and tackle pulled the chain through 20 m with a force of 1600 N. Use the expression

$$\text{work done} = F.s$$

to calculate the work done by the mechanic in pulling the chain with force *F* through distance *s*.

c) Use the expression

$$\% \text{ efficiency} = \frac{\text{work done (output)}}{\text{energy supplied (input)}}$$

to calculate the percentage efficiency of the block and tackle.

d) What is the main cause of the low efficiency?

e) Explain why it is useful in this case to have such a low efficiency.

8 A heat engine works on the principle that some of the heat produced by a source can be converted into mechanical work:

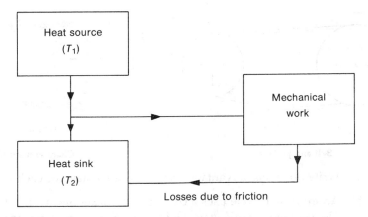

The theoretical efficiency of the heat engine is given by the expression

$$\% \text{ efficiency} = \frac{T_1 - T_2}{T_1} \times 100 \quad (T \text{ in kelvins})$$

a) How is the high 'source' temperature achieved in a motor car engine?

b) What is the 'heat sink' referred to in the diagram?

c) Taking the external temperature to be 20 °C (293 K), calculate the theoretical efficiency of a heat engine with the following inlet (source) temperatures:

   i) 100 °C (373 K)
   ii) 1000 °C (1273 K)

d) In practice the efficiency of a heat engine operating at 1000 °C is approximately 50% at best. Compare this with your answer to part c) ii) and account for any difference.

e) Why is it not possible to operate a heat engine at temperatures much above 1000 °C?

9 a) Use the formula

$$\text{power} = \frac{\text{energy transferred or work done}}{\text{time taken}}$$

to calculate the power developed during each of the following examples:

   i)   A girl running steadily to the top of a flight of stairs in 30 s. She gains 4000 J of potential energy.
   ii) An electric bar heater which releases 60 kJ of energy in 1 min.
   iii) A pulley which raises a load of 1000 N through 2 m in 5 s.
   iv) A space probe radio which radiates 12 J in 1 min.
   v)   The Sun, which releases 1.2×10^{34} J in 1 year.

b) A light bulb is marked 60 W. Explain what this means.

10   Rotary motion can be transferred from one shaft to another using a belt on pulley wheels or a sprocket and chain system.

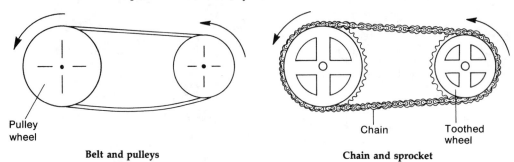

Pulley
wheel

Chain

Toothed
wheel

Belt and pulleys   **Chain and sprocket**

a)   Write down *one* advantage and *one* disadvantage of each mechanism.

b)   An exercise bicycle uses a chain and sprocket mechanism to drive a flywheel. The user must work against a frictional force which can be varied by adjusting the tension in the steel band. (See the diagram on the next page.)

    i)   Explain why the sprocket and chain mechanism is the better choice for use on the exercise bicycle.

   ii)   List *two* safety problems that might arise when using the cycle. What modifications would make it safer to use?

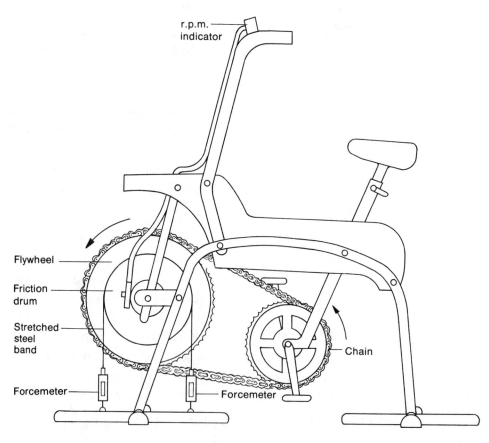

r.p.m.
indicator

Flywheel

Friction
drum

Stretched
steel
band

Forcemeter

Forcemeter

Chain

iii) How can the frictional force be calculated from the readings on the force-meters?

iv) What measurements must be taken, in addition to the friction applied, in order to calculate the energy transferred during a period of exercise on the machine?

c)   A chart on the cycle can be used to convert the value of the frictional force applied (N) and revolutions per minute (r.p.m.) of the flywheel into power output (W). Part of the chart is shown below, with one of the values omitted.

Frictional force (N)	Power output (W)	
	40 r.p.m.	80 r.p.m.
20	16	32
40	32	
60	48	96
80	64	128
100	80	160

i) What is the power output needed to maintain 80 r.p.m. against a frictional force of 40 N?

ii) How much energy is transferred when cycling for 1 min at 80 r.p.m. against a frictional force of 40 N?
(Formula: energy transferred = power output × time.)

iii) Calculate the circumference of the flywheel friction drum.
(Formula: work done = force × distance.)

2 HEAT

Conduction, Convection and Radiation

1 Match the methods of heat transfer with their correct definitions, and write out the correct table.

Method of heat transfer	*Definition*
Conduction	The transfer of energy by circulation of the material due to differences in temperature.
Convection	The transfer of energy by means of electro-magnetic waves without the need of a material medium.
Radiation	The transfer of energy through a material, from points of high temperature to points of low temperature, without the movement of the material itself.

2 Copy the diagram of a vacuum flask and explain carefully how the design of the flask prevents heat transfer between the contents of the flask and the surroundings.

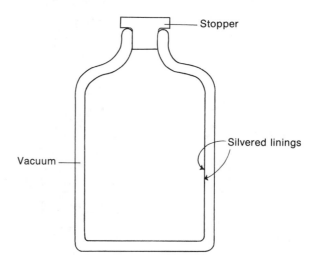

3 Explain the following observations.

a) Feathers and fur are very good at keeping birds and animals warm.

b) The cooling unit is placed at the top of a freezer, but the heating element in a water tank is at the bottom.

c) It is more comfortable to wear white clothes in the summer than black clothes.

d) People suffering from hypothermia are wrapped in a plastic sheet coated with shiny aluminium.

e) In cold conditions it is better to wear several layers of thin clothing rather than one layer of thick clothing.

f) Newspaper used to keep fish and chips hot will also keep ice cream cold.

g) A fire fighting suit is bright and shiny.

h) The inside of a greenhouse is warmer than the outside.

i) Food in a chest freezer will stay frozen even if the lid is left open for several hours. Food in an upright freezer will soon begin to defrost if the door is left open.

j) During vigorous exercise your face becomes very red.

4 The list below shows the specific heat capacity of some materials.

Material	Specific heat capacity (J/kg/°C)
Air	900
Alcohol	2500
Aluminium	900
Copper	400
Cotton	1400
Glass	670
Ice	2100
Iron	450
Polystyrene	1300
Water	4200

a) Explain the term 'specific heat capacity'.

b) What units is specific heat capacity measured in?

c) i) Draw a column graph of the specific heat capacities given in the list above.

   ii) Which material needs the most energy to warm it up through a given temperature change?

   iii) Which material is the easiest to warm up through a given temperature change?

d) How much energy would be needed to warm up
   i) 3 kg of water by 10 °C?

   ii) 500 g of aluminium from 20 °C to 50 °C?

5   The diagram below shows some of the main energy losses from a home in Britain.

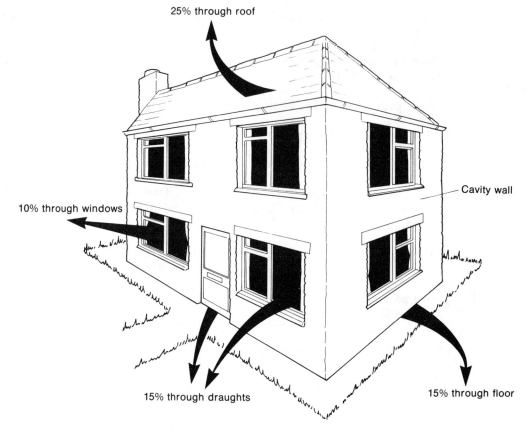

25% through roof

Cavity wall

10% through windows

15% through draughts

15% through floor

a)   Energy is also lost through the cavity walls.

    i)   What percentage is this of the total energy loss?

    ii)   Explain how filling the cavity with foam reduces heat loss.

b)   Suggest *two* reasons why the rooms on the north side of the house may be colder than those on the south side.

c)   The owner of the house decides to improve insulation by either fitting double glazing or insulating the roof.

    i)   Which of the two methods would save more on fuel bills? Explain your answer.

    ii)   What additional benefit would be gained from fitting double glazing?

d)   Explain how each of the following reduces fuel costs:

    i)   fitting aluminium foil behind radiators

    ii)   blocking off unused fire places and their chimneys

    iii)   lagging the hot water cylinder

    iv)   laying carpets

e)   Explain why energy conservation is an important issue on a global scale.

6   Electric storage heaters operate on cheap electricity supplied at night, which is used to heat concrete blocks. During the following day, heat stored in the blocks is transferred to the room.

Concrete is a suitable material for this application because it has a high density and is good at storing thermal energy. The energy stored in warming 10 kg concrete through 1 °C (costing 0.01 p) will raise the temperature of 1 m³ of air by 7 °C. If the concrete was replaced by the same mass of water, however, the energy stored in raising the water temperature by 1 °C (costing 0.03 p) would raise the temperature of 1 m³ of air by 35 °C.

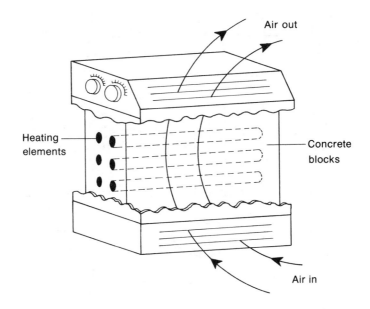

An electric storage heater

a)   Explain why electricity is cheaper at night.

b)   The larger the specific heat capacity of a material, the better it is at storing thermal energy. Would you expect concrete to have a larger specific heat capacity than water? Explain your answer.

c)   Using the formula

$$\text{mass} = \text{volume} \times \text{density}$$

calculate the volume occupied by 10 kg concrete (density 2400 kg/m³).

d)   Use the same formula to calculate the volume occupied by 10 kg water.

e)   Give *two* reasons why water is not used in preference to concrete in electric storage heaters.

f)   Do storage heaters warm a room mainly by conduction, convection or radiation?

Latent Heat

1 25 cm^3 of ethanol was placed in a boiling tube fitted with a side-arm. An immersion heater was placed in the tube, which was fitted inside a polystyrene jacket as shown in the diagram.

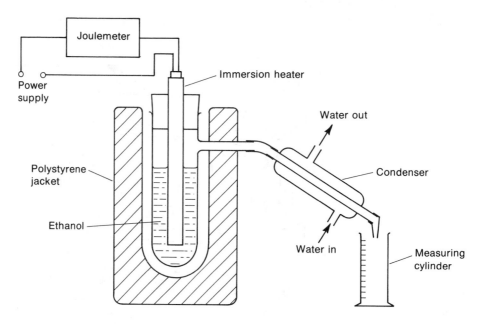

Once the ethanol was boiling at a steady rate, a 10 cm^3 measuring cylinder was placed under the delivery bend to collect ethanol from the condenser. During the time that 5 cm^3 of ethanol was collected, the joulemeter showed that 3.5 kJ of electrical energy was supplied to the heater.

a) Why was the boiling tube placed inside a polystyrene jacket?

b) If the density of ethanol is 0.8 g/cm^3, calculate the mass of 5 cm^3 of ethanol. (Formula: mass = volume × density)

c) The mass of one mole of ethanol is 46 g. Calculate the heat of vaporisation of ethanol in kJ/mol.

d) i) Why was collection of ethanol *not* begun as soon as some ethanol began to flow out of the condenser?

   ii) Write down two sources of error in this experiment, and state how the method could be modified to reduce them.

e) Would you expect the value for the heat of vaporisation of ethanol obtained from this experiment to be greater or less (numerically) than the true value? Explain your choice.

2 Halocarbons are compounds containing carbon bonded to elements in group 7 of the Periodic Table, the halogens. Some are used as refrigerants, dry cleaning solvents and aerosol propellants. An immersion heater was placed into a beaker containing a liquid halocarbon of formula $C_2Cl_3F_3$. The temperature of the liquid was taken every 30 seconds. The results obtained were as follows:

Time/s	Temperature/°C
0	16
30	19
60	23
90	27
120	31
150	35
180	39
210	43
240	47
270	47
300	47
330	47
360 (heating stopped)	47

a) What was the temperature in the laboratory at the start of the experiment?

b) What is the boiling point of the halocarbon?

c) For how long was the halocarbon boiling?

d) A joulemeter in the heating circuit showed that the heater was supplying energy at a rate of 2400 joules per minute. How much energy was transferred to the halocarbon while it was boiling?

e) During the time the halocarbon was boiling, 37.50 g were vaporised.

   i) What is the relative molecular mass of the halocarbon?

   ii) How many moles of halocarbon were vaporised?

   iii) Calculate the energy required to vaporise 1 mole of the halocarbon.

f) Why has the use of halocarbons as refrigerants and aerosol propellants been considerably reduced?

(Relative atomic masses: $C = 12$, $F = 19$, $Cl = 35.5$)

3   A sample of ice was taken out of a freezer at $-10\ ^{\circ}C$ and left to stand in a container in the kitchen sink. The temperature in the kitchen was $21\ ^{\circ}C$. Every 2 minutes the temperature of the ice was taken, until no further change took place.

   a)   Sketch the graph you would expect to obtain if temperature (y-axis) was plotted against time (x-axis) for the results of this experiment. Add labels to show the melting point of ice and room temperature.

   b)   i) Mark a point 'X' on your graph where the kinetic energy of the water molecules is increasing.

         ii) Mark a point 'Y' on your graph where the potential energy of the water molecules is increasing.

        iii) Mark a different point 'Z' on your graph where the molecules are capable of vibrational movement only.

4   Explain with reasons, whether a burn caused by steam at $100\ ^{\circ}C$ would be more or less serious than a burn from water at $100\ ^{\circ}C$, all other factors being the same.

3 LIGHT

Shadows and Mirrors

1 Copy and complete these sentences about light, choosing words from this list to fill in the blanks:

> **energy**   **illuminated**   **luminous**   **reflect**   **straight**
> **wavelength**

a) Light is a form of _____.

b) Light is a wave motion with a _____ of about 0.0005 mm.

c) Objects that produce their own light are called _____ sources.

d) Other objects are _____ by this light and _____ it into our eyes.

e) Light travels in _____ lines.

2 a) Copy the diagram below which shows a ray being reflected by a plane mirror.

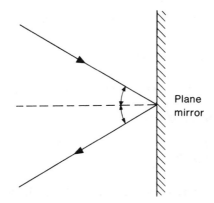

Plane
mirror

b) i) Add labels to your diagram for the following:
Incident ray
Reflected ray
The normal

ii) What is the relationship between these three?

c) i) Add labels to your diagram for the following:
Angle of incidence
Angle of reflection

ii) What is the relationship between these two?

3   A child, one metre in height, is standing one metre away from a torch and one metre in front of a wall, as shown in the diagram.

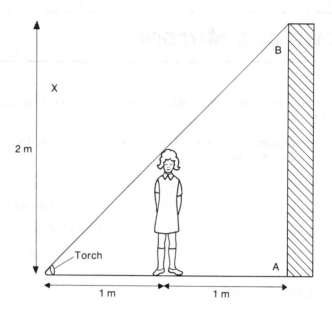

a)   How tall is her shadow?

b)   If a second torch is shone from the position marked 'X', 1.5 metres above the ground, what would happen to the darkness of the shadow at
   i) point A?
   ii) point B?

c)   Why is the shadow of a person standing under a street lamp not sharp?

d)   What is meant by
   i)   the umbra
   ii) the penumbra?

e)   Why is it better to have classrooms lit by long fluorescent lamps than single small lamps?

4   a)   List *three* ways to describe the image of a plane mirror.

b)   **POLICE**

   If you see this in the rear view mirror of your car, what is actually written on the front of the police car?

c)   Show how two plane mirrors can be used to produce a periscope.

5 a) Copy diagrams A and B and complete them to show how the parallel rays of light are reflected by the two mirrors.

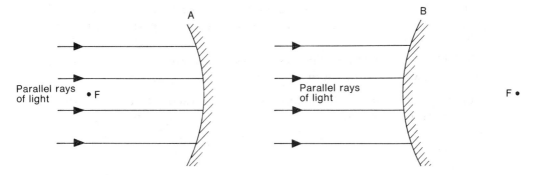

b) Copy these sentences choosing only the correct alternatives from inside the brackets.

   i) A mirror that curves in is called a (concave/convex) mirror and is a (diverging/converging) mirror. Mirror A is (concave/convex).

   ii) A mirror that curves outwards is a (concave/convex) mirror and is a (diverging/converging mirror). Mirror B is (concave/convex).

c) Mark on each of your diagrams A and B

   i) the focal length

   ii) the centre of curvature

d) Which type of mirror would be used as a driving mirror? Explain your answer.

Refraction and Lenses

1 Match the words in the left-hand column with the definitions in the right-hand column.

Words	*Definitions*
Refraction	Light rays 'bouncing back' from a surface.
Dispersion	The bending of light when it passes from one optical medium to another.
Reflection	The splitting up of white light into the colours of the rainbow.

2 a) Copy these sentences choosing only the correct alternatives from inside the brackets.

   i) Rays of light travelling from air into glass are bent or refracted (towards/ away from) the normal. This is because air is optically (less/more) dense than glass.

   ii) Rays of light travelling from glass into air are bent or refracted (towards/ away from) the normal.

b) Copy and complete the following diagrams to show the approximate direction of the refracted rays.

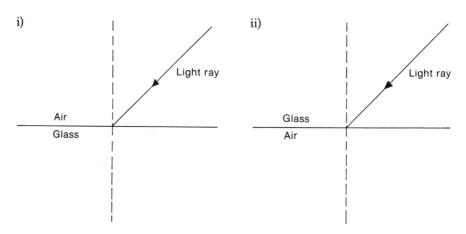

i)

ii)

3 a) Copy the diagram below.

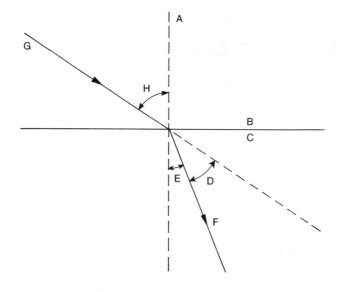

b) Copy the following list of terms and say which letter on the diagram belongs to which term.

>   **Optically less dense medium**
>   **Optically more dense medium**
>   **Incident ray**
>   **Refracted ray**
>   **Normal**
>   **Angle of incidence**
>   **Angle of refraction**
>   **Angle of deviation**

4 The refractive index of glass is 1.5, showing that the speed of light in a vacuum is 1.5 times greater than the speed of light in glass.

$$\text{refractive index of glass} = \frac{\text{speed of light in a vacuum}}{\text{speed of light in glass}}$$

$$= \frac{300\ 000\ \text{km/s}}{200\ 000\ \text{km/s}}$$

$$= 1.5$$

The diagram shows how a ray of light behaves on passing from a vacuum into a block of glass.

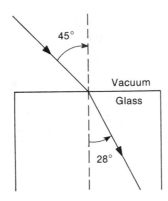

a) Calculate $\dfrac{\sin 45°}{\sin 28°}$ using a pocket scientific calculator, and comment on the result.

b) Draw diagrams showing what would happen to a ray of light on entering a vacuum from a block of glass as shown opposite. Find any unknown angles by calculation.

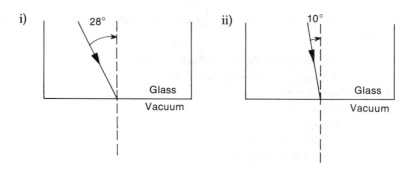

i)   28°   ii)   10°

Glass   Glass
Vacuum   Vacuum

c)   The refractive index of water is 1.33 ($\frac{4}{3}$). Calculate the speed of light in water. (Speed of light in a vacuum = 300 000 km/s.)

5 a)   Copy and complete the ray diagram to show how a swimming pool appears shallower than it really is, owing to refraction of light at the surface.

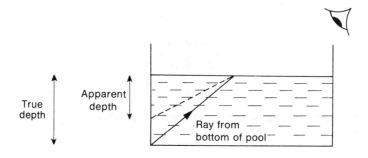

True depth   Apparent depth   Ray from bottom of pool

b)   Explain how a rod appears to bend when partly immersed in water. You may wish to copy and amend the following diagram to help explain your answer.

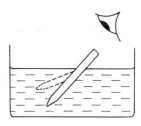

c)   A coin is placed on the bottom of a plastic cup. An observer stands above and to one side of the cup so that the coin is just hidden behind the rim. Draw a diagram showing this, and which also explains how the coin becomes visible when the cup is carefully filled with water, even though the observer does not move.

6 A swimming pool appears to be 1.5 m deep. If the refractive index of water is 1.33 ($\frac{4}{3}$), what is the real depth? Show your working.

7   A plastic block was placed on the bottom of a ripple tank so that water just covered the block.

This wave pattern was obtained.

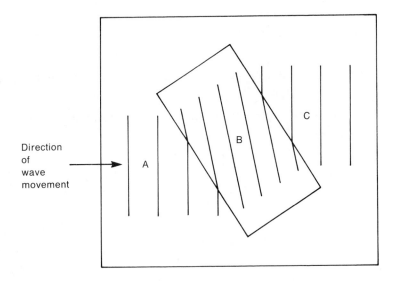

a)   Explain how the waves in a ripple tank are produced.

b)   The waves in the region A were travelling at 10 cm/s.
     What happens to the speed of the waves in regions B and C?

c)   Which behaviour of waves does this experiment demonstrate? Choose from the following list:

     reflection   diffraction   dispersion   refraction

8   The power of a lens is measured in dioptres (D):

$$\text{power of lens (D)} = \frac{1}{\text{focal length (m)}}$$

The power of a convex lens is positive, while that of a concave lens is negative.

a)   What is the focal length of a lens?

b)   Calculate the focal length, in centimetres, of lenses with the following powers.

     i) $+0.5$ D
     ii) $+20.0$ D
     iii) -1.5 D

c)   Which of the lenses in part b) could be used as a magnifying glass?

9

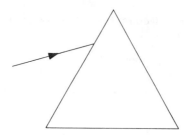

a) Copy and complete the diagram above to show how the prism **refracts** and **disperses** light.

b) Copy and complete the diagram below to show how internal reflection occurs in a prism.

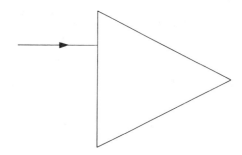

c) i) Explain how two prisms can be used to make a periscope.

   ii) Why is it better to use prisms than plane mirrors?

10 a) Copy diagrams A and B and complete them to show how the parallel rays emerge from each lens.

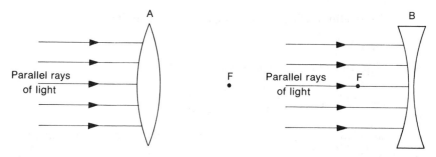

b) Copy these sentences choosing only the correct alternatives from inside the brackets.

   i) A lens which is thicker at the centre than at the end is called a (concave/convex) lens and is a (converging/diverging) lens. Lens A is a (concave/convex) lens.

   ii) A lens which is thinner at its centre is called a (concave/convex) lens and is a (converging/diverging lens). Lens B is a (concave/convex) lens.

c) Mark on your diagrams the **focal length** of each lens.

11   The power of a lens is measured in dioptres (D):

$$\text{power of lens (D)} = \frac{1}{\text{focal length (m)}}$$

The power of a convex lens is positive, while that of a concave lens is negative.

a)   What is the focal length of a lens?

b)   Calculate the focal length, in centimetres, of lenses with the following powers.

    i)   +0.5 D

    ii)   +20.0 D

    iii)   −1.5 D

c)   Which of the lenses in part b) could be used as a magnifying glass?

Diffraction and Dispersion

1 a)   Copy the diagram below, which shows how a prism produces a continuous (rainbow) spectrum from white light, and add the missing colours.

Yellow
Green

b)   Which colour of the rainbow corresponds to light with the longest wavelength?

c)   The diagram shows how a rainbow is formed by raindrops.

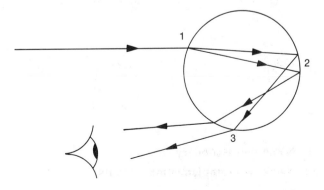

i) Will the rainbow be visible looking towards or away from the Sun?

ii) As shown, will the rainbow have red or violet at the top?

iii) At which of the points 1, 2 and 3 does **refraction** occur?

iv) At which of the points 1, 2 and 3 does **reflection** occur?

2 A thermometer with its bulb painted black is placed just beyond the red region of the continuous (rainbow) spectrum produced from sunlight using a prism.

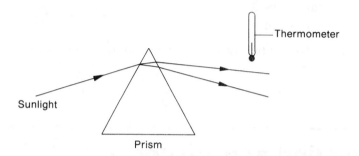

What would happen to the reading on the thermometer, and why?

3 Three projectors are pointed at a white screen. The projectors are equally bright. One has a red filter attached, the second has a green filter and the third a blue filter. A student looks at the screen. The colours he sees are shown in the diagram.

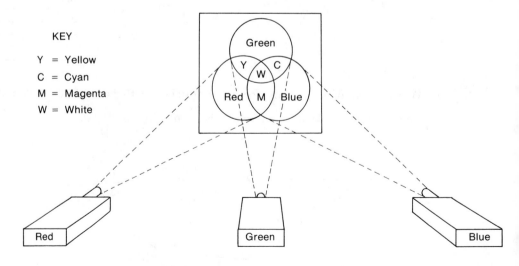

KEY

Y = Yellow
C = Cyan
M = Magenta
W = White

a) i) Name two **secondary** colours.

ii) Name two **complementary** colours.

b) Use the results from this experiment to predict the colour seen on the screen in the following examples. The filters used are shown.

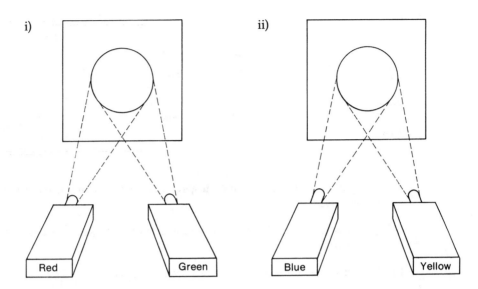

i)

ii)

Red   Green   Blue   Yellow

Optical Devices

1 Which of the optical components listed would be suitable for the following applications? A different component is required for each application.

> convex lens   convex mirror   concave mirror   parabolic mirror
> concave lens   plane mirror

a) a shaving mirror

b) a telescope mirror

c) a wide-field security mirror in a shop

d) a magnifying glass

e) a correcting lens for short-sight

f) a periscope

2 The pin-hole camera (below) can be used to take photographs without using a lens.

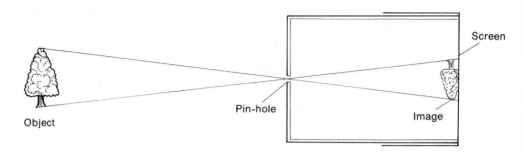

a) Copy and complete the following sentence by choosing the correct word from the brackets.

The image formed by a pin-hole camera is (real/virtual) and upright/inverted).

b) Describe *two* ways of making the image bigger.

c) State *two* effects on the image of making the pin-hole larger.

d) Why are pin-hole cameras rarely used to take photographs?

e) During a partial eclipse of the Sun, small images of the 'crescent' of the partially eclipsed Sun can be seen in the shadow beneath a leafly tree. Explain this observation.

3 The diagram shows a screen with a lens in front of it. In front of the lens is a flower.

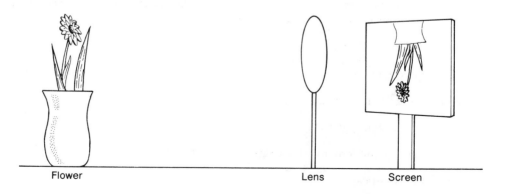

a) The image of the flower on the screen is fuzzy. Suggest *two* ways in which you could make the image sharp.

b) Once the image is sharp, the flower is moved a little way towards the lens. What must you now do with the screen to make the image sharp again?

c) What difference would you see in the image if the lens was replaced by another of the same power, but with only half its diameter?

d) With the help of a diagram, explain how the lens could be used together with a lightproof box and photographic film to make a simple camera.

4

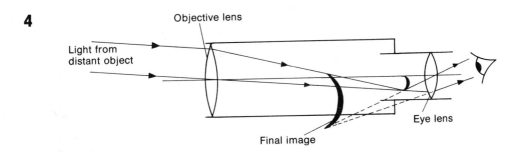

The above diagram shows the arrangement of lenses in a telescope. This type is known as a refractor.

a) Which of the two lenses has the longer focal length?

b) Is the image formed by the eye lens real or virtual?

c) How is the telescope focused?

d) How could the final image be made upright?

e) Why are the final images in **astronomical telescopes** inverted and not corrected as in part e)?

f) Which of the following features of the telescope determines the faintest object the telescope will reveal?

    A. Focal length of the objective lens.

    B. Focal length of the eye lens.

    C. Diameter of the objective lens.

    D. Diameter of the eye lens.

g) What is used to gather light in a reflecting telescope?

5 The diagram shows how a single convex lens can be used as a magnifying glass.

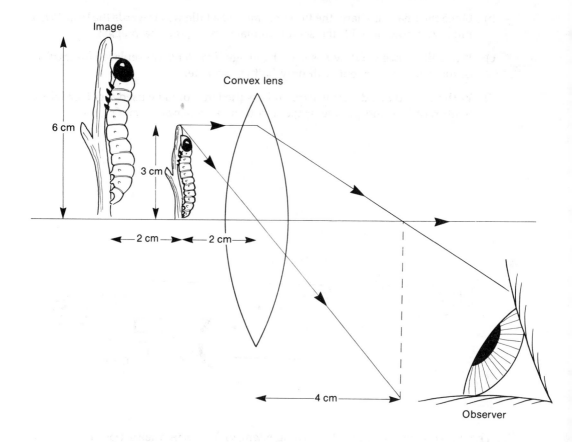

a) What is the focal length of the lens?

b) On a copy of the diagram, extend the rays backwards to show how the eye sees an enlarged image of the object.

c) Would it be possible to obtain an image of the enlarged view on a piece of white card? Explain your answer.

d) What magnification has been given in this experiment?

6 The diagram shows two solid glass rods, similar to optical fibres. Both are of the same type of glass and are surrounded by air.

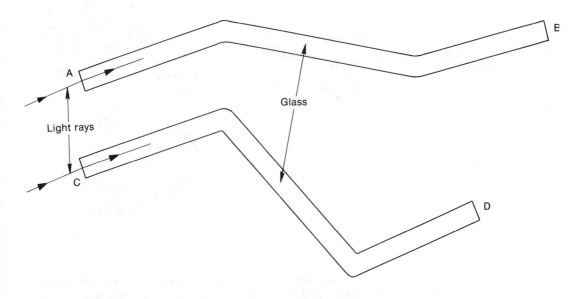

a) It is found that the ray of light entering the rod at A reaches B, but the ray entering the rod at C does not reach D. Explain why.

b) Copy the first diagram and complete it by showing how the light ray travels from A to B.

c) Light takes 10^{-3} s to travel 2×10^5 m along an optical fibre. Use these figures to calculate the speed of the light in glass.

d) The speed of light in a vacuum is 3×10^8 m/s. Explain any difference between this value and the speed of light in glass.

7 Read the passage below and answer the questions which follow.

Optical fibres are used in medicine. Mounted in a device called an endoscope they can be used to examine the inside of the alimentary canal. A bronchoscope can be used to examine the respiratory passages and lungs. The diagram opposite shows an endoscope.

In the coherent bundle, optical fibres are arranged so that they have exactly the same positions at both ends of the bundle allowing an image to be transmitted. The ends of the bundle are evenly cut and polished and each fibre carries a small part of the image. In the incoherent bundle the fibres are arranged randomly. This allows light to be sent down the tube but no image can be seen.

The endoscope will also include a channel which allows water to be passed down to clean the lens. Other channels may also be present, for example one which allows biopsy probes to be put into the body. These are used to remove small samples of tissue for testing.

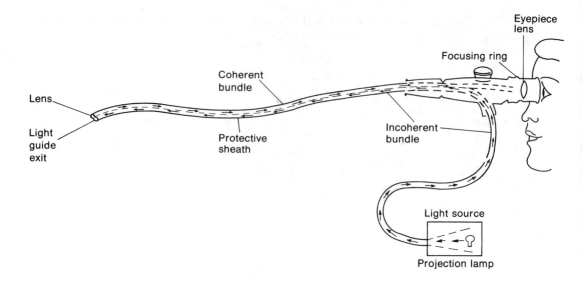

The end of the endoscope tube is flexible and can be moved around inside the body. There is no heat produced at the tip, since the source of light is at the other end.

a) Name *two* medical instruments which involve the use of optical fibres and say what they are used for.

b) How are the optical fibres arranged in
  i) a coherent bundle?
  ii) an incoherent bundle?

c) Why are both types of fibre bundle used in these medical instruments?

c) Why is it important to keep the lens clean?

e) Suggest one medical condition which may be diagnosed using an endoscope.

f) What is the advantage of
  i) the end of the tube being flexible?
  ii) no heat being produced at the tip?

g) What is a biopsy?

h) Briefly describe one other, non-medical, use of optical fibres.

Electromagnetic Radiation

1   The electromagnetic spectrum is shown below. Some types of wave have been left
out.

Radio.		Infra-red	Visible light		X-rays	
	A			B		C

a)   Name the missing waves in boxes A, B and C.

b)   Which of the waves has the longest wavelength?

c)   Which of the waves has the lowest frequency?

2   One type of wave has a wavelength of 2000 m. 150 000 complete waves pass a point
every second.

a)   What is the frequency of the wave (give the unit)?

b)   Work out the speed of the wave (give the unit).

c)   Name *two* types of wave that human sense organs detect.

d)   Name *two* types of wave that human sense organs cannot detect.

3   a)   Place the following regions of the electromagnetic spectrum in order of
increasing wavelength.

ultraviolet   radio waves   visible light   X-rays
infra-red   gamma rays

b)   Correctly match each region of the spectrum with an application.

Region of spectrum	*Application*
Visible light	Sun beds and sun lamps
Radio waves	Sterilising pre-packed hospital equipment
X-rays	Finding people buried in collapsed buildings
Gamma rays	Communication over long distances
Ultraviolet	Laser surgery
Infra-red	Diagnosing broken bones

4 a) Explain what is meant by saying that the waves from a source are **plane-polarised**.

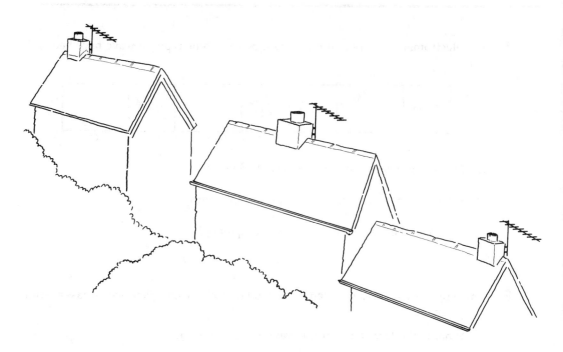

b) The TV aerials on the houses in a street are arranged as shown in the diagram.

i) The aerials all point in the same direction. What are they pointing to?

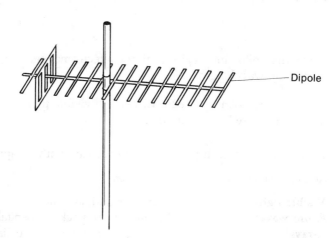

Dipole

ii) Explain why the aerials are **all** arranged so that their **dipoles** are in the same plane in each case.

5 Some dyes used to stain biological specimens for microscopic examination are fluorescent. They absorb ultraviolet light and emit visible light. The diagram represents a ray of ultraviolet radiation. (1 nm = 0.000 000 001 m)

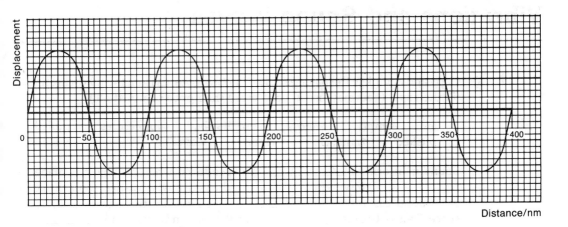

a) What is the wavelength, in nm, of this radiation?

The diagram below represents the visible spectrum.

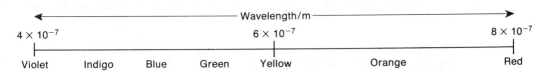

b) The ultraviolet light in part a) was absorbed by a dye and visible light was emitted. If the wavelength of the emitted radiation had increased by a factor of 5 estimate the colour of the light produced.

c) An object appears yellow when viewed under white light. It appears red when viewed under red light and it appears black when viewed under blue light. Explain why.

4 SOUND

Vibrations and Sound Waves

1 a) Copy and complete the passage below choosing words from the following list to fill the gaps. (You may use a word more than once or not at all.)

> air   empty   energy   longitudinal   molecules   pulled
> pushed   transverse   vibrate   waves

> Sound is a form of _____. It is produced when an object is made to _____. It travels in _____ through any substance, solid, liquid or gas. Sound can travel through _____ but not through _____ space. This is because _____ in the air can be made to _____. The molecules are alternately _____ together and _____ apart to form the sound _____. Sound waves are examples of _____ waves.

b) Explain why astronauts in space cannot talk directly to each other but must communicate by radio.

c) Through which type of substance, solid, liquid or gas, does sound travel most quickly? Give a reason for your answer.

d) Try to explain how the beating of a drum produces sound waves in the air.

2 The diagram below shows the sound waves produced by a vibrating tuning fork.

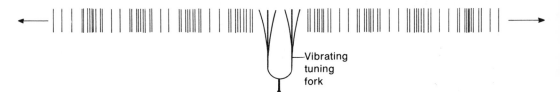
Vibrating
tuning
fork

a) Copy the wave pattern on one side of the tuning fork.

b) Mark
   i) a point A where the air is compressed
   ii) a point B where the air is rarefied
   iii) a distance C which represents the wavelength of the sound

c) The diagrams below represent the air molecules at the points A and B you have marked.

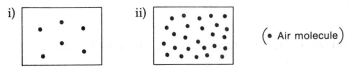

Copy the diagrams and say which point A or B they represent.

d) Copy the statement below, choosing only the correct alternative i), ii) or iii) to complete it.

When a sound wave passes by, in this direction →, an air molecule

  i) oscillates at right angles to the direction of the wave ●↕

  ii) oscillates in the same direction as the wave motion ●↔

  iii) moves with the wave ●→

3 Copy these sentences, choosing only the correct alternative from inside the brackets.

a) When the (amplitude/frequency) of vibrations increases, the sound produced becomes (louder/softer).

b) When the (amplitude/frequency) of vibrations increases, the pitch of the sound becomes (higher/lower).

c) When the frequency of vibrations is (changing/constant) a sound is heard as a musical note with a fixed (loudness/pitch). For example, middle C has an (amplitude/frequency) of 256 vibrations per second (Hz).

4 Sound level is measured in units called **decibels** (dB). The table below shows the approximate sound level of some sources of noise, measured at a 'working' distance.

Source	Sound level (dB)
Minimum sound that can be heard	0
Whisper	30
Conversation	60
Heavy traffic	90
Pneumatic drill	100
Low flying jet aircraft	130
Pain threshold	140
(At 100–110 dB conversation becomes impossible.)	

a) Using the information in the table to help you, estimate the sound level of

  i) a telephone ringing

  ii) a loudspeaker at a disco

  iii) a person shouting at the top of his voice

b) In schools close to busy airports, lessons are frequently disrupted by the noise from low flying aircraft. Describe one way of soundproofing classrooms against this noise.

5 If a sound level is higher than 80 dB, the ears may be damaged.

Kate wants to find out how far away from a noisy machine she can sit for a long time without risking damage to her ears. She took sound level meter readings at different distances from the machine. These are her results.

Distance (m)	1	2	3	5	7	8	10	14
Sound level (dB)	96	90	86	82	89	78	76	73

a)   i) Plot a graph of these results. Label the axes as shown.

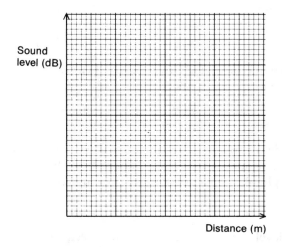

ii) Kate has made a mistake in one of her readings. Which one is incorrect?

iii) Suggest what you think the reading on the sound level meter should have been at that point.

b) Use the graph to answer the following questions.

i) What is the sound level 4 m from the machine?

ii) How far away from the machine is the sound level 74 dB?

iii) What is the closest Kate can sit to the machine and know that her ears will not be damaged?

6 The noise level and how long it lasts affects whether our hearing may be damaged by noise. Workers in noisy conditions are protected by law. At 90 dB the maximum exposure time allowed is eight hours. At 93 dB it is four hours and at 96 dB it is two hours.

a) What would you expect the time limit to be at 99 dB?

b)   i) Workers on a production line in a large factory claimed that the noise levels they were exposed to were a danger to health. If you were the safety officer for the factory, how would you decide whether or not their claim was correct?

    ii) How can workers in noisy conditions be protected against damage to their hearing?

c)   The sound from personal stereos goes directly into the ear. Measurements of the sound level produced by them, at full volume, gave the following results:

> Pop music (Jason Donovan)   110 dB
> Heavy metal music (Jon Bonjovi)   100 dB
> Classical music (Tchaikovsky)   110 dB

    i) Should the manufacturers of personal stereos issue a health warning with each one? If so, what should it say?

    ii) What modifications could be made to personal stereos to reduce any risks?

7   a)   What is an echo?

    b)   Explain why echoes are a nuisance in large concert halls but can sometimes improve the sound in a small concert hall.

    c)   As part of the planning for a large concert hall experiments were carried out to determine how much sound energy was absorbed by brick, carpet and tiles at various frequencies. The results are given below.

Material	Percentage of sound energy absorbed at a certain frequency		
	125 Hz	500 Hz	2500 Hz
Brick	0.05%	0.02%	0.05%
Tiles	0.8%	0.5%	0.7%
Carpet	0.17%	0.8%	0.9%

    i)   Which material is the best absorber at a frequency of 125 Hz?

    ii)   Which material is a better absorber at a frequency of 125 Hz?

    iii)   If 100 J of sound energy of frequency 500 Hz hits the wall covered with tiles, how much sound energy is reflected?

    d)   Why do you think such experiments were carried out?

    e)   Why are wires sometimes stretched across concert halls?

8 The note played by a football referee's whistle is shown as a wave on an oscilloscope using a microphone.

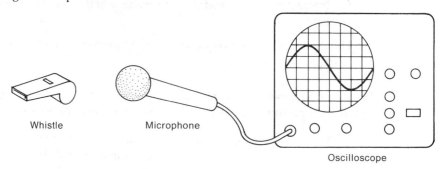

Whistle   Microphone

Oscilloscope

a) Copy the diagram of the oscilloscope screen and draw in the trace you would expect to see if the same note was obtained but the note was quieter than before.

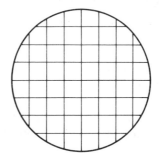

b) On a second copy of the diagram draw in the trace you would expect to see if a dog whistle was blown, which produced a note equally loud but with a frequency four times greater.

Vibrations and Musical Instruments

1 The vibrator produces a wire vibration pattern as shown below.

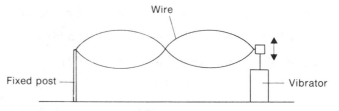

Wire

Fixed post ─   Vibrator

Draw the pattern produced when:

a) The frequency of vibration is doubled.

b) The amplitude of the vibration is doubled.

c) The string is vibrating at its fundamental frequency.

d) Describe the effect of each of the changes in parts a), b) and c) on

    i) the pitch of the note produced by the wire

    ii) the loudness of the note produced by the wire

2 Musical instruments produce a note when something is made to vibrate. Match the instruments a)–e) below with their vibrating parts.

Instrument	*Vibrations occur in*
a) **Violin**	a metal rod
b) **Triangle**	a reed
c) **Drum**	air
d) **Flute**	a skin
e) **Saxophone**	strings

3 When air is blown through the opening at the bottom of an organ pipe, it strikes a sharp edge and a vibration is set up in the air inside the pipe. The loudness of the note produced can be changed by changing the diameter of the pipe, while the pitch of the note depends on the length of the pipe.

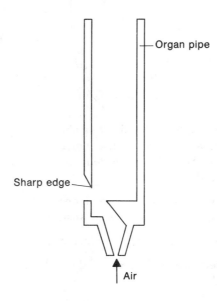

a) Copy and complete the following table showing the effect of a change in the diameter of the pipe on the amplitude, frequency and speed of the sound wave produced.

Change	Effect of the change on the sound wave		
	Amplitude	Frequency	Speed
Increase in pipe diameter			
Decrease in pipe diameter			

b) Would you expect the note produced by a shorter pipe to have a higher or lower pitch? Explain your answer.

4 a) It is easy to recognise sound from different instruments. For example a violin and a piano sound different, even if they are playing the same note. Explain why this is so. In your answer you need to refer to the quality of sound, waveform and harmonics. Use diagrams if you wish.

b) In a violin the strings are mounted on a hollow box. The air in the box vibrates as the strings vibrate and so does the box. Explain what effect this has on the sound produced.

c) Why are low pitched musical instruments usually larger than high pitched ones?

5

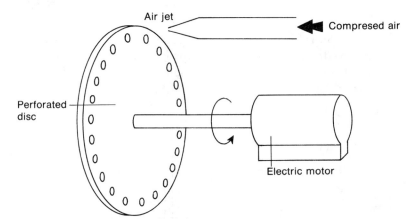

A siren can be produced by directing a jet of compressed air at a set of perforations around the edge of a rotating disc. The air is forced through each hole in turn and produces a series of pulses. The frequency of the note depends on the time interval between the pulses.

a) Would you expect an increase in the rotation rate to produce a note of higher or lower frequency? Explain your answer.

b) Suggest one other method of increasing the frequency of the note.

c) What effect would increasing the velocity of the air jet have on the note produced?

6   A singer, singing a note at a particular frequency, may cause a wine glass to break. Explain how **resonance** causes this to occur.

7   A thin metal plate is supported at its centre from below. A small amount of sand is sprinkled on its surface, and a violin bow drawn down the middle of one edge while the plate is touched at one corner and one-quarter of the way in from the corner as shown in the diagram. The sand gathers into the pattern shown and a note is heard.

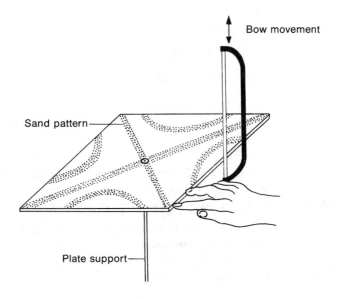

a)   What causes the note?

b)   Explain why the sand gathers at certain regions on the plate.

c)   Suggest one method of making the note louder.

d)   A modified experiment is shown below.

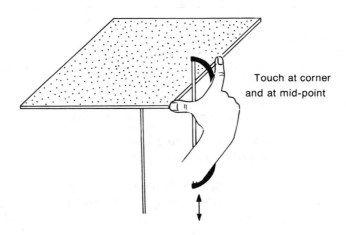

Which of the following is most likely to be part of the pattern formed?

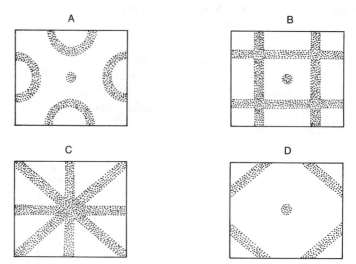

6 Two guitar strings, A and B, are stretched across the same pair of bridges as shown. A small V-shaped piece of card is placed over the centre string B. The tension in each string can be varied using keys at one end of the wires.

When string A is plucked, nothing happens to string B. The tension in string A is adjusted and the string is plucked once more. This process is repeated until, at one particular tension setting, string B begins to vibrate when string A is plucked. The piece of card is thrown off string B.

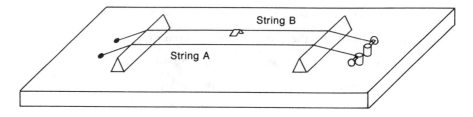

a) Copy the diagram

b) How is the vibration of one string transmitted to the other?

c) Choose the correct word or words from the list provided to complete the following discussion of this experiment. Write out the completed passage.

> **resonance   vibration   energy transfer   forced vibration
> natural frequency**

The _____ of string B in response to vibrations in string A is an example of _____. When string A vibrates at the _____ of string B, _____ occurs and _____ between the strings is very efficient.

Audio Devices

1 The diagram below is of a **moving coil microphone**. Study the diagram, then copy and complete the passage which follows about how the microphone works. Choose words from the list to fill in the blanks.

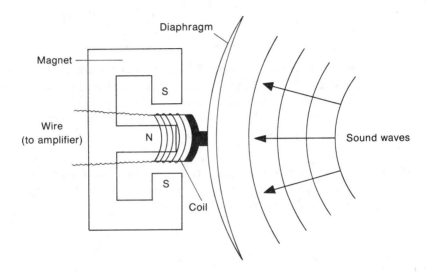

| alternating | vibrate | magnetic | loudspeaker |
| frequencies | ear-drum | coil | |

The diaphragm of the microphone corresponds to the _____ in the human ear. When sound waves reach the microphone, the diaphragm begins to _____. The coil moves back and forth in the _____ field. A small _____ current is induced in the wire of the _____. When amplified, this current can be used to reproduce the sound using a _____. The moving coil microphone can respond to _____ of sound between 20 Hz and 20 000 Hz, the limits of human hearing.

2 a) Copy the following sentences, choosing only the correct alternatives from inside the brackets.

   i) In a microphone, (electrical/sound) energy is converted into (electrical/sound) energy.

   ii) In a loudspeaker, (electrical/sound) energy is converted into (electrical/sound) energy.

   b) Draw a diagram of a moving coil loudspeaker. Label the magnet, coil, cone and wire from the amplifier.

c) Why do speakers in hi-fi systems, such as the one shown below, often have one small and one large loudspeaker in the same unit?

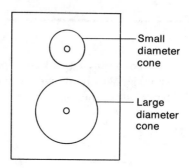

Small diameter cone

Large diameter cone

d) Mr Smith went to a specialist hi-fi shop to buy a pair of loudspeakers. He was prepared to pay a lot of money for a pair with a good bass response. However, the manager of the shop advised him that expensive loudspeakers, able to give notes down to 30 Hz, would be ineffective in his small sitting room. Was this good advice? Explain your answer.

3 One type of telephone earpiece contains a disc, clamped round its edge, with the poles of a magnet close to its centre. Wires carrying the incoming electrical signal are wrapped round the poles of the magnet.

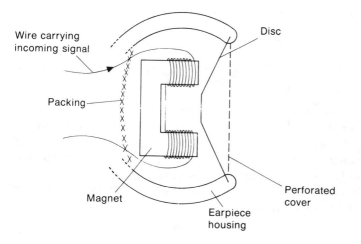

Wire carrying incoming signal

Packing

Magnet

Disc

Perforated cover

Earpiece housing

When the current in the wire changes, the degree of magnetisation changes. The disc vibrates as the force of attraction towards the magnet varies rapidly. This reproduces the speech which gave rise to the signal in the wires. An absorbent material is packed behind the disc.

a) Suggest a suitable material for the disc.

b) What is the purpose of the packing material?

c) What type of current – alternating or direct – is present in the coil?

d) Explain how sound produced by the disc in the unit travels to the ear of the listener.

4 Explain how sound waves are converted into an electrical current by the carbon microphone in the mouthpiece of a telephone.

5 Thousands of kilometres of copper cable carry telephone messages all around the world, but there are problems associated with the use of this network. Using optical fibres to transmit telephone calls can overcome some of these problems.

a) Who invented the telephone and when?

b) Give *one* use of the telephone network in addition to transmitting conversations.

c) Copy and complete the following table which compares the use of optical fibres and copper cables for transmitting telephone messages.

Copper cables	*Optical fibres*
Message carried as an electrical signal Copper is very expensive The signal can be upset by electrical interference from nearby wires Fewer messages can be sent down one wire (low signal rate) Cables are heavy and occupy a great deal of space The signal weakens and needs amplifying about every 2 km Cables are easy to join Cables are not easily broken	

6 A room contains two loudspeakers as shown in the diagram. The loudspeakers are supplied by the same signal generator and operate in phase, producing a note in the audible range.

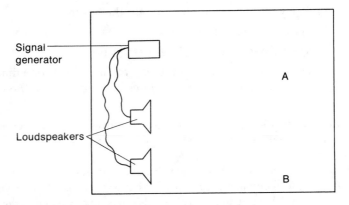

Describe what you would hear when walking from A to B, and explain your answer.

Applications

1

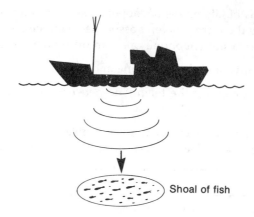

Shoal of fish

The diagram above shows a fishing boat using echo-sounding to detect a shoal of fish. A short pulse of high frequency sound waves is emitted from the boat, and the echo from the shoal is detected 0.1 s later. Sound waves travel through sea water at 1500 m/s.

a) How far below the boat is the shoal of fish? Show your working.

b) Describe two other situations in which a ship may use echo-sounding.

c) Why is high frequency sound used?

d) How might a geologist use echo sounding?

2 a) What is ultrasound?

b) Find out how ultrasound is used in the following situations and explain *two* of them:

  i) by bats and dolphins to help them 'see'

  ii) in spectacles for blind people

  iii) to detect flaws in pieces of metal

  iv) to remove particles of solid material, which sometimes develop into painful stones such as kidney stones, without cutting the patient.

3 Read this passage about the use of ultrasound in pregnancy and answer the questions which follow.

> Ultrasound can be used to produce pictures of unborn babies. This is often referred to as a scan. An ultrasonic transmitter/receiver (the transducer) is moved across the mother's abdomen. This sends ultrasound waves into the body in a narrow beam. Some of the ultrasound is reflected when it comes to a material through which it would have a different speed. The bigger the difference in speed, the bigger the

amount of reflection. The receiver changes the reflected waves back into electrical energy and displays them as a spot on an oscilloscope screen. The position of each spot depends on the time delay between the wave being sent out and the reflected wave being received. These spots are built up into a picture on the screen. The pictures enable the size of the baby to be measured. The size of the head is a useful way of determining the baby's age. Abnormalities in the developing skeleton can also be seen. At the lower power levels used, ultrasound has no known harmful effect on any part of the body.

a) For what reasons is a scan usually carried out?

b) Why is ultrasound preferred to X-rays for producing such pictures?

c) How are the ultrasound waves generated?

d) Why are some of the waves reflected?

e) What type of machine is used to display the pictures?

f) The table below gives some information about the speed of sound in different materials.

Material	Speed of sound (m/s)
Muscle	1580
Soft tissue	1500
Bone	4100
Air	340
Saline gel	1515

i) Which one of the following places would cause most reflection of ultrasound?
A Where soft tissue meets muscle
B Where muscle meets bone
C Where saline gel meets soft tissue

ii) The diagram below shows the arrangement normally used for producing ultrasound pictures. Why must the transducer be 'coupled' to the patient's skin by the saline gel?

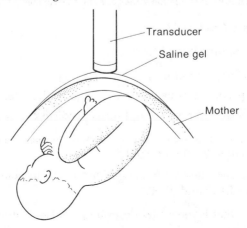

5 ENERGY RESOURCES

Fuels

1   The graph below shows a 'depletion curve' for world reserves of coal, an important
fossil fuel.

Consumption (10^9 tonnes per year)

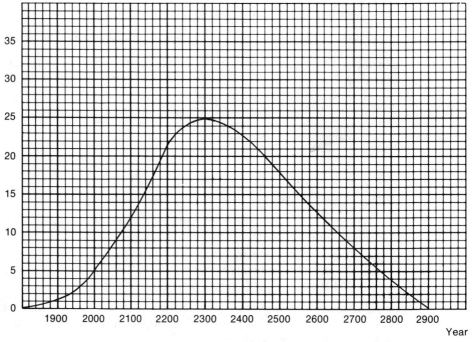

World consumption of coal in thousands of millions of tonnes per year for the period 1900–2900

a)   What is a fossil fuel?

b)   Name *two* other fossil fuels.

c)   Use the graph to find:

   i) the predicted consumption of coal in the year 2000

   ii) the year when consumption is predicted to reach a maximum value

d)   i) Give *one* reason for the predicted increase in coal consumption between
   the years 2000 and 2100

   ii) Give *one* reason for the predicted fall in coal consumption between the
   years 2400 and 2500.

e)   Explain what is meant by describing coal as a 'non-renewable' energy source.

2 Read the passage below and answer the questions which follow.

> Electric vehicles are rarely seen on our roads, with the exception of milk floats. Although the efficiency of a typical electric car (70%) is greater than that of a petrol vehicle (25%), the 'energy density' of lead/acid batteries used in electric cars is only 140 kJ/kg compared to 46 MJ/kg for petrol. To overcome this disadvantage, a new low-mass sodium/sulphur battery has been developed which is capable of storing the same amount of energy even though it has only 20% of the mass of the lead/acid type. The vehicles involved differ in mass also, since electric motors are up to five times heavier than the equivalent petrol variety. However, electric cars are believed to be less harmful to the environment as they do not release nitrogen oxides into the atmosphere.

a) Write down *two* advantages of electric cars over petrol cars, and *one* disadvantage.

b)   i) Explain what 'energy density' means.

   ii) What are the energy densities of electric and petrol cars as measured in J/kg?

   iii) What is the energy density of a sodium/sulphur battery, measured in kJ/kg?

c) In spite of being much less efficient, petrol vehicles can travel much further on one tank of petrol than an electric vehicle can on one charge. Why is this?

d) How long would it take to charge a 480 kJ capacity electric vehicle on a 240 V/5 A supply?

   (Electrical energy transferred, E, is found from the expression

$$E = ItV$$

   where I is the current (A), t is the time (s) and V is the voltage (V).)

e) Give *two* reasons why electric vehicles are suitable for use as milk floats.

f) Describe *one* consequence of the release of nitrogen oxides into the atmosphere.

g) It has been said that electric vehicles transfer their pollution to the power stations. Explain this statement.

Renewable Energy Resources

1 Read the passage which is about energy from biomass and answer the following questions.

> With fossil fuels running out, the world needs renewable energy sources that can be re-made as fast as they are used up. Plant material called **biomass** is a good renewable energy source.
>
> Biomass energy is particularly important in developing countries, which often do

not have their own fossil fuels and cannot afford to buy them. Examples of biomass fuels are wood, charcoal, alcohol, vegetable oil and biogas (methane).

A tenth of the energy stored by the process of photosynthesis could provide all the world's energy needs.

a)   What is the ultimate source of energy in the world?

b)   What is a renewable energy source?

c)   What is biomass?

d)   Give *four* examples of biomass fuels.

e)   Why is biomass energy particularly important in developing countries?

f)   Why are tropical countries generally better able to produce biomass fuels than cool countries like Britain?

2   Read this short passage about the production of biogas, then answer the following questions.

When vegetable and animal matter rots in the absence of air, a gas is given off. The gas is usually about 60% methane, the rest being mostly carbon dioxide. This biogas is a good fuel, particularly for cooking, heating and lighting in the home.

Rubbish is often tipped into holes in the ground. This is called landfill. This rubbish will also generate biogas.

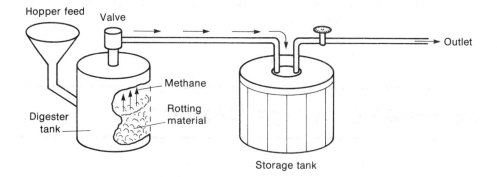

a)   Why is the gas called biogas?

b)   Why is biogas particularly easy to make on farms?

c)   What use can be made of the solid material left behind in the digestor?

3 Wind-powered electric generators (aerogenerators) are used to produce energy on a small scale at remote sites, or in an emergency when the main source of electricity fails. At present, the blades of a wind-powered generator can be up to 50 metres in diameter and the electrical power produced can reach up to 1 000 000 watts in favourable conditions.

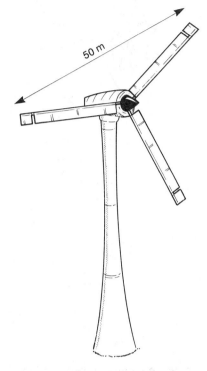

50 m

An aerogenerator

a) Which of the sites 1–3 shown on the map opposite would be suitable for an aerogenerator?

b) i) A conventional power station has an output of 2 000 000 000 W. How many aerogenerators would be needed to produce this amount of power?

ii) What effect would this number of aerogenerators have on the area in which they were built?

iii) Give *two* reasons why aerogenerators are not used for large scale electricity production in Britain.

c) What device could be used to convert the energy of the blades into electricity?

d) i) Explain why it is less harmful to the environment to generate electricity from 'alternative' energy sources such as wind power than from fossil fuels burnt in conventional power stations.

ii) Briefly describe the use of geothermal energy and one other alternative energy source.

4 The table below shows the energy consumption in millions of joules per passenger per kilometre for various types of transport.

Type of transport	Energy consumption (MJ/passenger/km)
Motorcycle (average)	0.72
Private car (average)	1.80
Bus	0.90
Diesel train	1.00

a) Which is the most energy efficient form of transportation?

b) List *two* factors which cause the energy consumption of private vehicles to be particularly variable.

c) What is the total energy consumption for transporting 20 people over a distance of 10 km using:

   i) 5 private cars?   ii) 1 bus?

d) Apart from energy conservation, give *one* other reason why the use of public transport should be encouraged.

e) Which would you expect to be more energy efficient, a ferry boat or an aeroplane, and why?

f) Explain how the shape of a vehicle can affect its energy efficiency.

5 The diagram shows a new idea for transferring energy from sea waves. An air-tight box is built on the edge of the sea. An entrance at the bottom of the box lets the sea flow in and out. At the top of the box is another opening which is connected to a turbine generator.

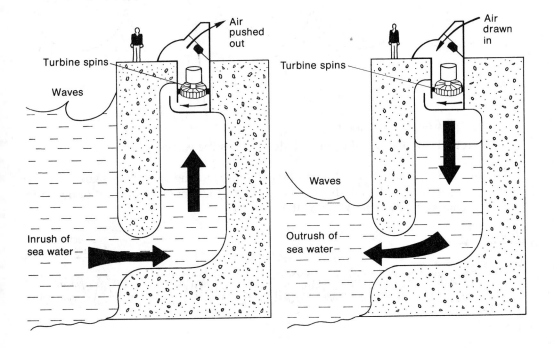

a) Explain, as fully as you can, how energy is transferred from the waves to produce electricity.

b) Part of the energy from the waves is not transferred into electricity. Suggest *two* reasons for this.

c) The turbine is specially made so that it spins in the same direction whether the air is going into or coming out of the box chamber. What advantage does this design have over a turbine that spins only when water is coming into the chamber?

d) Suggest *one* advantage and *one* disadvantage of building such a device on a coast where there are very large waves.

e) List *two* advantages that a generator powered by waves has over one that uses a fossil fuel.

6 WAVE MOTIONS

1 The diagram below shows a ship at anchor in rough seas. The water waves are transverse waves.

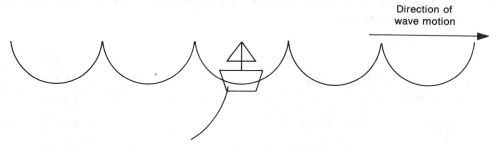

a)   i) Copy the diagram.

ii) Describe how the ship would move as the waves go by.

b) The diagram below shows a long spring vibrating along its length. This is an example of a longitudinal wave. Describe the motion of the part of the spring marked with a black dot as the waves go by.

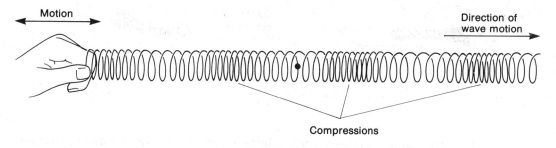

2 Copy the diagram of a wave in a length of rope and add labels which identify the wavelength, the amplitude and a wave crest.

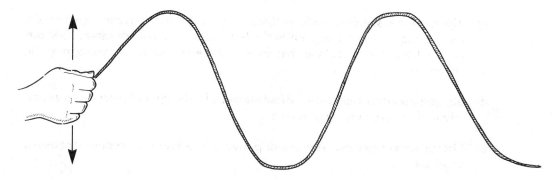

3 Copy and complete the following diagrams of ripple tank experiments to show the wave patterns produced as the experiments progress:

a)

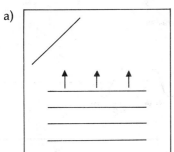

e)

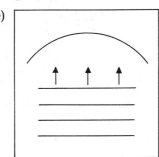

b)

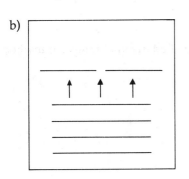

f)

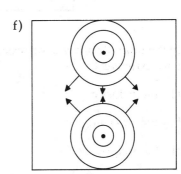

c)

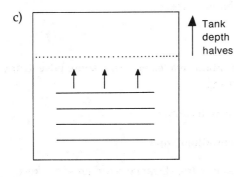

Tank
depth
halves

g)

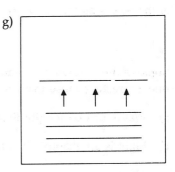

d)

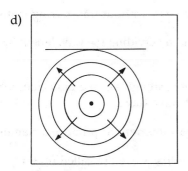

4   Water waves travel more slowly in shallow water.

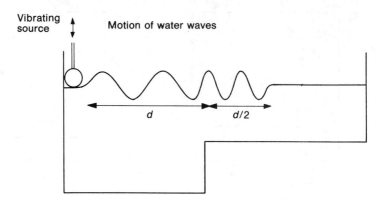

In the example shown, the distances travelled in equal times are marked. Describe what happens to

a)   the velocity

b)   the wavelength

c)   the frequency

d)   the amplitude

of the waves as they enter the shallow water.

5   Some of the following statements about waves are true, some false. Copy out each one, correcting those that are wrong.

a)   Waves can be longitudinal or transverse.

b)   Light is an example of a longitudinal wave.

c)   The amplitude of a water wave is the distance from crest to crest.

d)   Waves are a means of transferring energy without transferring matter.

e)   The frequency of a wave can be found by dividing the wavelength by the wave velocity.

f)   In the passage of a longitudinal wave through air, the molecules vibrate in a direction parallel to the direction of wave travel.

g)   Two progressive transverse waves can interfere to produce a standing wave.

h)   Points of zero displacement in a standing wave are called nodes.

6 Copy and complete the wave formula:

$$\text{velocity} = \underline{\hspace{3cm}} \times \text{wavelength}$$

Use it to carry out the following calculations.

a) Find the velocity of sound waves in air which have a frequency of 900 Hz and a wavelength of 0.35 m.

b) Calculate the wavelength of sound waves in water, having a frequency of 700 Hz and velocity of 1.43 km/s.

c) Find the frequency of sound waves in a steel rod, if the waves have a wavelength of 10 cm and travel at 5.5 km/s.

d) Calculate the wavelength of red light which has a frequency of 5.0×10^{14} Hz and velocity 3.0×10^8 m/s.

e) Calculate the time interval between waves on a surfing beach if the waves have a wavelength of 48 m and travel at 6 m/s.

f) Find the wavelength of radio waves with frequency 5×10^8 Hz and velocity 3×10^8 m/s.

7 Select one of the wave phenomena below which is responsible for each effect described in a)–e).

reflection   **refraction**   **diffraction**

a) Two parallel rays of light are brought to a focus by a convex lens.

b) An echo is heard when a gun is fired at some distance from cliffs.

c) Light from the Sun remains visible for a short while after the Sun has set below the horizon.

d) Circular waves are produced when parallel water waves meet a barrier with a small central slit.

e) When a source of white light is viewed through a glass plate on which fine lines have been etched (say 80 lines per millimetre), a series of rainbow patterns can be seen.

Theme 5

Electricity and Magnetism

1 ELECTRICITY

Static Electricity

1   The diagrams below show one method of charging a gold leaf electroscope using a positively charged rod.

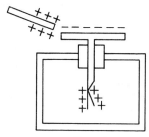
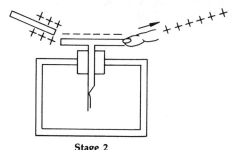

Stage 1	Stage 2	Stage 3
Rod brought close to plate	With rod in place the plate is earthed	First the finger and then the rod are taken away

a)   Copy the diagrams and add the third one to show what happens when the finger and rod are removed.

b)   Suggest what the rod could be made of and describe one way of charging it.

c)   Draw another set of diagrams to show how the same rod can be used to introduce the opposite electrical charge.

d)   A gold leaf electroscope is given a positive charge. When a charged rod is brought towards the cap of the electroscope, the deflection of the leaf increases. What charge was present on the rod? Explain your answer.

e)   A charged electroscope left in a room for several days slowly loses its charge and the deflection of the leaf falls to zero. Explain this observation.

2   Explain each of the following:

a)   It is difficult to keep

i) gramophone records, and   ii) television screens, free of dust

b)   You can make a balloon stick to the ceiling after rubbing the balloon on your clothing.

c)   In dry weather, people walking on nylon carpets may get a shock if they touch a metallic object.

d)   A mirror which has been polished with a dry cloth, on a dry day, soon becomes very dusty.

3 An aircraft is flying above an electrically charged thunder cloud as shown in the diagram.

   a) Copy the diagram and draw in the positions and signs of any charges induced in the aircraft.

   b) Will these induced charges be present when the aircraft eventually lands at its destination, well away from the storm? Explain your answer.

   c) Why is it unlikely that any passengers in the aircraft will be harmed as a direct result of the aircraft being struck by lightning?

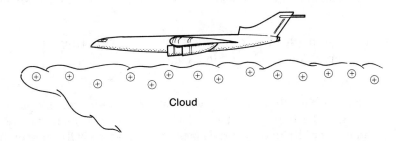

Cloud

   d)   i) After flying through air for some time in fine weather, a helicopter must be earthed while hovering before ground personnel attach any cargo to the underneath of the helicopter. Why is this necessary?

      ii) How would you earth the helicopter safely?

4

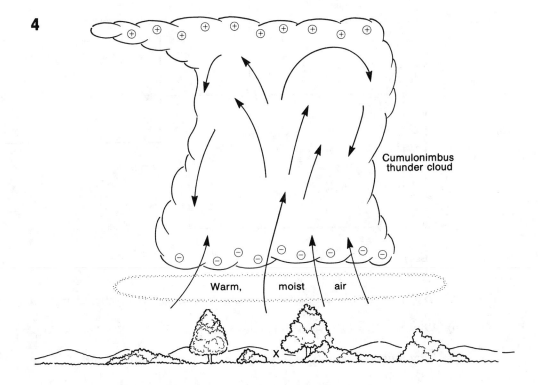

Cumulonimbus thunder cloud

Warm,   moist   air

The diagram opposite shows the air currents in a typical thunder cloud (cumulonimbus). Charges are generated within it, producing lightning.

a) What sign of charge would be induced on the ground at X?

b) Explain how a lightning stroke produces thunder.

c) Under what conditions is the flash of lightning seen at the same time as the thunder clap is heard?

d) The speed of sound in air is 300 m/s. The speed of light in air is 300 000 000 m/s. If a thunder clap is heard 5 seconds after the lightning flash, how far away is the storm?

e) Use the words CONVECTION and FRICTION to explain how charge separation occurs within a cumulonimbus cloud.

5 The experiment below shows that an electric current is a flow of electric charge. The dome and base of a Van de Graaf generator are connected to an ammeter by a pair of charged plates. A polystyrene ball coated with aluminium paint hangs between the plates. When the generator is running, the ball oscillates between the plates, making contact with one then the other, and the ammeter registers a reading.

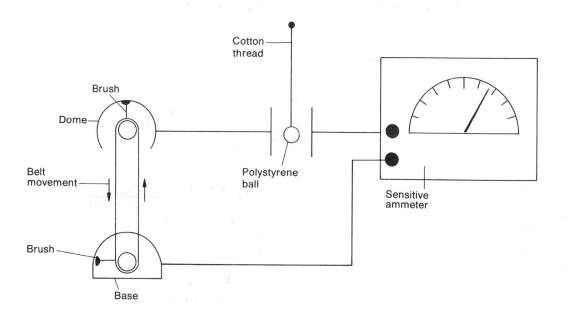

a) Explain how the Van de Graaf machine produces an electric charge.

b) Why does the ball oscillate between the plates?

c) Why must the polystyrene ball be coated in aluminium paint?

d) Copy the following explanation of what is happening in the experiment. Choose words from this list to complete it:

   ammeter   electric   flow   plates

   The moving ball passes _____ charge between the two _____ and the charge travels round the circuit. As the charge passes through the _____ it registers the _____ of electric charge.

e) Explain why
   i) The ammeter reading increases if the plates are moved closer together.
   ii) The ammeter reading falls to zero if the ball is prevented from moving.

f) If the ball makes contact with each plate twice every second, and transfers 0.000 001 coulombs each oscillation, calculate the current flowing through the ammeter.

$$\left(\text{Formula: current (A)} = \frac{\text{charge transferred (C)}}{\text{time (s)}} \right)$$

Conduction and Resistance

1

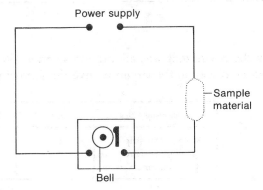

a) Which of the following materials would conduct electricity well and cause the bell to ring when placed in the circuit shown above?

   polythene rod   glass rod   sulphur crystal   iron bar
   block of wood   copper wire   aluminium foil   zinc rod
   rubber band   nickel spatula

b) Name one solid, non-metallic element which conducts electricity.

2   The metal strip and wires shown in the diagram were connected one by one into the circuit drawn below.

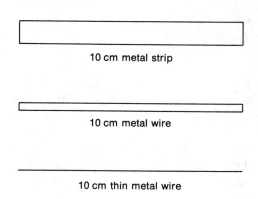

10 cm metal strip

10 cm metal wire

10 cm thin metal wire

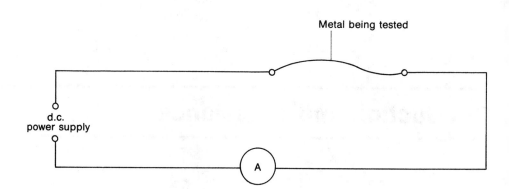

Metal being tested

d.c.
power supply

A

a)   Copy the circuit diagram, adding the symbol (V) to show how a voltmeter would be placed in the circuit to give the following results.

Metal being tested	Current (A)	Voltage (V)
10 cm metal strip	5	1.5
10 cm metal wire	4.5	1.5
10 cm thin metal wire	4.2	1.5

b)   i)   What is the effect of using thinner wire in this circuit?

     ii)   If a current of 5 A was passed through *each* wire, which would produce the most heat?

c)   If each strip is made of the same metal, which one has the highest resistance?

Circuits

1 a) Name the components shown below.

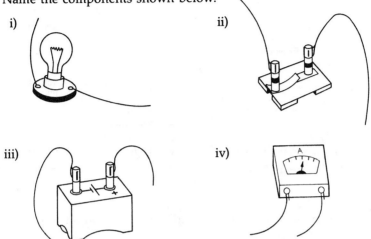

i)

ii)

iii)

iv)

b) These components could be used to make an electrical circuit for lighting up a small cupboard. Draw such a circuit, using the standard symbols for each component.

2 The diagram shows a resistor and an ammeter connected to a power supply.

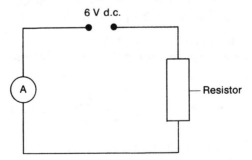

6 V d.c.

A

Resistor

a) Copy the diagram.

b) Copy the sentences below choosing only the correct alternatives from inside the brackets.

   i) When the p.d. of the power supply is increased, the reading on the ammeter (increases/decreases).

   ii) When the current flowing through the resistor increases, its temperature (increases/decreases).

3 a) Suggest where in the home it is a good idea to have two separate switches controlling the same light. Such an arrangement of switches is shown in the circuit diagram below.

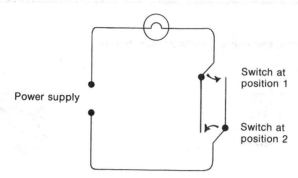

Power supply

Switch at
position 1

Switch at
position 2

b) Design a circuit which will allow a light to be turned on or off from three positions independently. Describe one situation where this would be useful.

4 Below are six statements about circuits. Sort them into two groups under the following headings:

Series circuits	Parallel circuits

There is only one path for the current.
There are several paths for the current.

The current is not the same at all points in the circuit.
The current is the same at all points in the circuit.

The p.d. across each component is the same.
The p.d. across each component is usually different.

5 a) Choose the accurate version of Ohm's law from the following list and copy it out:

A The potential difference across a conductor is equal to the resistance of the conductor (in ohms) divided by the current flowing through it (in amperes)

B The current flowing through a metal conductor is directly proportional to the potential difference across its ends at constant temperature.

C The resistance of a conductor is found by dividing the current flowing through it into the potential difference across its ends.

D A metal conductor has a resistance of 1 ohm if a current of 1 ampere flows through it when a potential difference of 1 volt is applied across its ends.

b) The graph below shows how the current flowing through a resistor changes as the potential difference across it is varied.

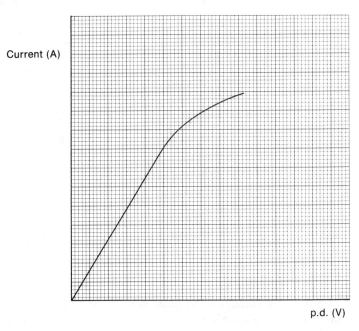

Current (A)

p.d. (V)

i) Copy the graph and label it to show the region where Ohm's law applies.

ii) At the point where the behaviour of the resistor begins to deviate from Ohm's law, does its resistance increase or decrease? Explain your answer.

iii) Suggest an explanation for the deviation from Ohm's law.

c) Measuring the resistance of a light bulb filament does not necessarily lead to a correct calculation of its power rating. Explain why.

6 What is the current shown on the ammeters a)–d) in each circuit shown below. All values are in amperes.

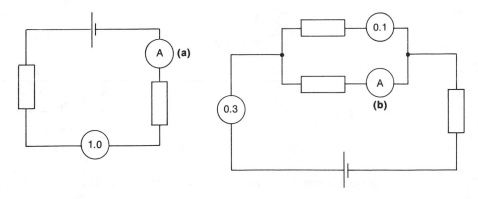

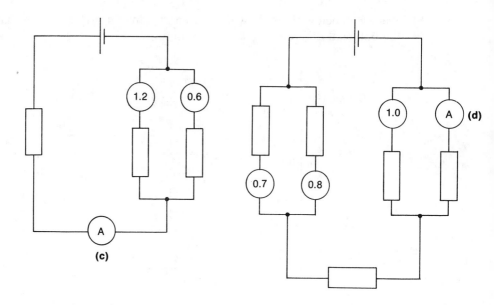

7 What are the readings on the ammeters a)–d) in the circuits shown below? All readings are in ampheres.

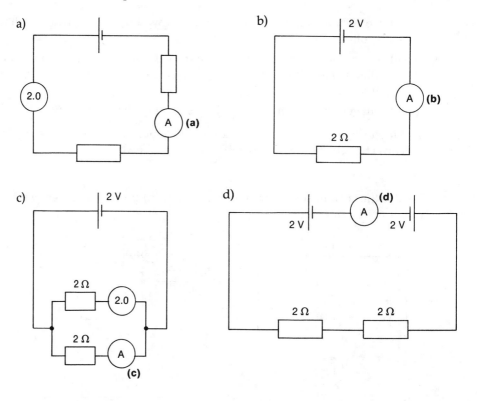

(Formula: p.d. across a component = current flowing × resistance of the component.)

8 The diagram below shows three cells connected in parallel.

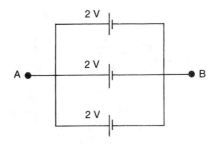

a) What would a voltmeter read when connected across the terminals A and B?

b) Give *two* reasons why it is better to use three cells in this way instead of just one cell.

c) Why should cells *not* be left connected in parallel when not in use?

9 Arrange the following circuits in order of increasing ammeter reading. All resistors, and all cells, are identical.

1.

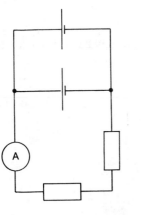

2.

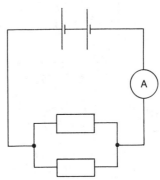

3.

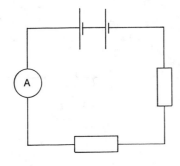

10 Copy the circuits a)–e) below. For each one give the correct voltmeter reading.

a)

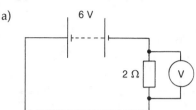

b)

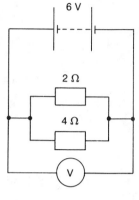

c)

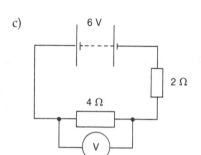

d)

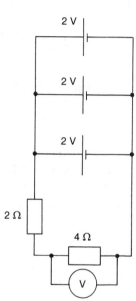

e)

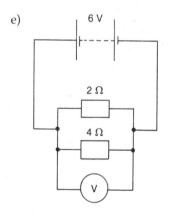

11 In 40 s a charge of 80 C leaves a cell and supplies 240 J of electrical energy to an appliance.

a) What is the cell p.d.?

b) What current was drawn from the cell?

$$\left(\begin{array}{l}\text{Formulae: charge} \;=\; \text{current} \times \text{time} \\ \text{cell p.d.} \;=\; \dfrac{\text{energy transferred}}{\text{charge}}\end{array}\right.$$

Electricity in Use

1

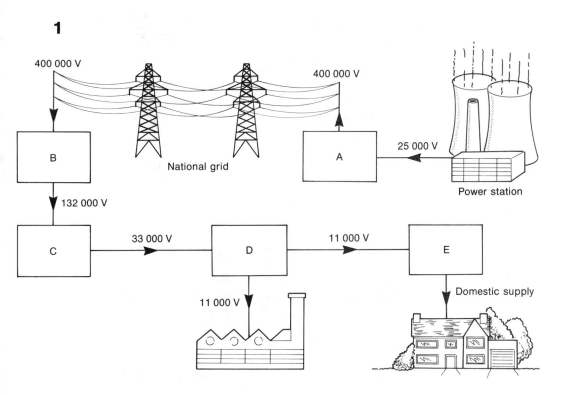

The diagram shows stages in the production and distribution of electricity, from power stations to homes and industry, via the national grid.

a)   What is the main advantage of the grid system?

b)   i) Why is power transmitted at a very high voltage?
      ii) Give *two* reasons why alternating current is essential for this network.

c)   Which of the transformers A–E are step-up transformers?

d)   What is the voltage of the domestic electricity supply?

e)   Why is aluminium preferred to steel for overhead power cables?

f)   Silver is one of the best metallic conductors of electricity.
      i) Give two reasons why thick silver cables would be an advantage in the national grid.
      ii) Give two reasons why silver is not used for overhead power cables.

2 If electricity costs 6.5 p per kWh, calculate

   a)   the cost of running a 2 kW bar heater for 8 hours

   b)   the charge for electricity used between the two meter readings below

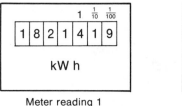

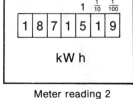

Meter reading 1   Meter reading 2

3 The diagram below shows a standard three-core flex plug.

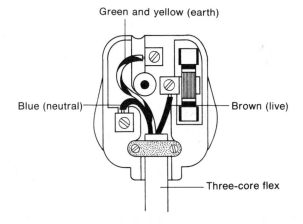

Green and yellow (earth)

Blue (neutral)

Brown (live)

Three-core flex

   a)   What is the purpose of the earth wire (green and yellow)?

   b)   What type of appliance needs to have an earth wire connected?

   c)   Why is the fuse connected into the live wire (brown)?

   d)   i) What happens to the fuse when an unusually large current flows through it?

        ii) How does the fuse protect an appliance?

   e)   Find out which domestic appliances must be protected by

        i) a 3 amp fuse

        ii) a 13 amp fuse

        (Give at least three examples in each case.)

   f)   If you are using an appliance and the fuse 'blows', what two actions should you take before using the appliance again?

4 Lisa has just bought a hair dryer. The diagram shows some of the parts inside it.

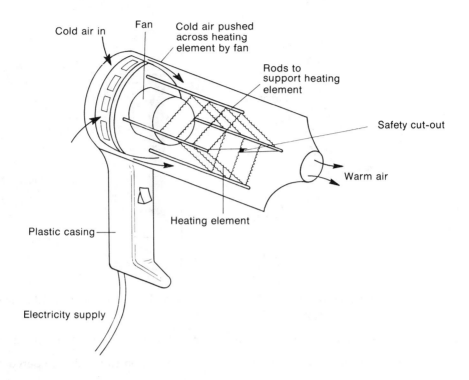

a) Explain why:

   i) the case is made of plastic and not metal

   ii) the heating elements are *not* made of carbon

b) The hair dryer has a label with the following information:

Power rating	720 W
Supply	240 V a.c.

   i) A power of one watt means that one joule of energy is transferred each second. How much energy is transferred by the hair dryer each second?

   ii) What is the current supplied to the hair dryer.

$$\left(\text{Formula: current} = \frac{\text{power}}{\text{voltage}}. \right)$$

c) Suggest why the hair dryer must not be used by someone having a bath.

d) The safety cut-out is a *bimetallic strip*. Explain how this device operates.

5 The diagram below shows the structure of an electrical cell used in a wide range of small appliances.

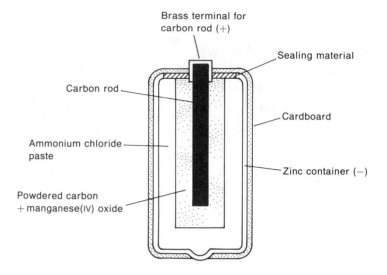

a) This type of cell is called a dry cell. Why is the ammonium chloride used in the form of a dry solid?

b) Write an ionic equation for the reaction at the negative terminal.

c) Suggest a reason for surrounding the carbon rod with powdered carbon.

d) The reaction at the positive terminal is

$$2NH_4^+(aq) + 2e^- \rightarrow 2NH_3(g) + H_2(g)$$

If bubbles of gas coated the carbon rod, the efficiency of the battery would be reduced. Explain how the two product gases, hydrogen and ammonia, are removed from the carbon rod.

e) The dry cell cannot be recharged. What is another disadvantage of a cell that has the negative terminal as the casing?

Cathode Rays

1 Some of the following statements about cathode rays are true, some are false. Copy out each one, correcting those that are wrong.

a) Cathode rays are emitted from a heated negative electrode.

b) Cathode rays are not affected by magnetic fields.

c) Cathode rays can pass through a thick metal plate.

d) A cathode ray is a beam of electrons.

e) Cathode rays are attracted to a negatively charged plate.

f) Oscilloscopes and televisions make use of cathode rays.

2 This question concerns the use of an oscilloscope as a voltmeter. The two traces below were obtained with the Y-gain set at 2 V/division.

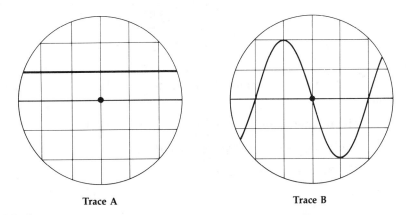

Trace A   Trace B

a) i) What type of voltage has been connected across the Y input to produce trace A?

   ii) What type of voltage has been connected across the Y input to produce trace B?

b) What is the reading shown by trace A?

c) What is the amplitude of the voltage indicated by trace B?

d) Draw the appearance of the screen for trace A after the time base has been switched off.

e) Which of the traces, A or B, could have been produced in each of the following experiments?

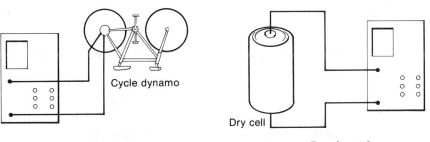

Experiment 1   Experiment 2

3   A 50 Hz a.c. supply is connected across the Y-input terminals of an oscilloscope, and the time base adjusted to give the trace shown below.

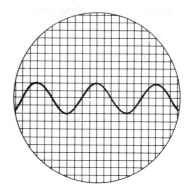

Draw the new appearance of the trace after the following changes have been made:

a)   The frequency of the input is changed to 100 Hz.

b)   The peak-to-peak voltage is halved.

c)   The time base is switched off.

4

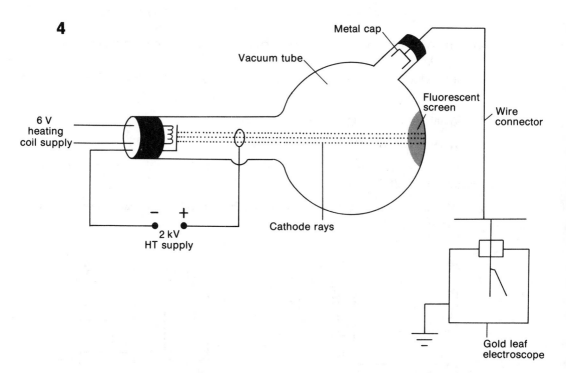

The apparatus above was used to demonstrate that cathode rays carry negative charge. The beam was deflected so that it hit the metal cap, which was connected to the plate of a gold leaf electroscope. The electroscope had been charged previously so that it carried a small negative charge, giving a small deflection of the leaf.

a) Describe briefly how a negative charge can be induced in an electroscope.

b) Why is the tube evacuated?

c) How could the beam be deflected so that it hits the metal cap?

d) If the cathode rays carry negative charge, what would you expect to see inside the electroscope when the cathode rays hit the metal cap?

e) Apart from carrying negative charge, list *three* properties of cathode rays.

5 The diagram opposite shows some components of a black and white television tube.

a) What is the function of the following items?
   i) the heater
   ii) the cathode
   iii) the anode
   iv) the coils
   v) the coating on the screen

b) The variable voltage on the modulator controls the number of electrons travelling towards the screen. What effect will this have on the appearance of the spot seen on the screen?

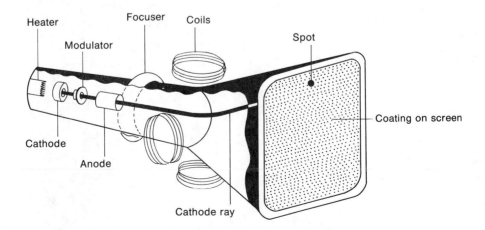

c) How does a colour television tube produce pictures which can show every colour of the spectrum?

6

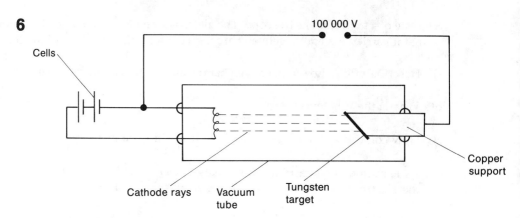

Which of the following are produced when cathode rays collide with the metal target in the apparatus shown above?

    A.   neutrons

    B.   alpha particles

    C.   x-rays

    D.   sound waves

    E.   protons

2 MAGNETISM

Permanent Magnets

1

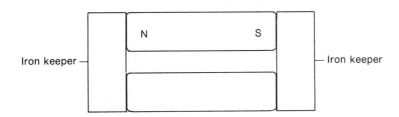

a) Bar magnets are frequently stored in pairs using iron 'keepers' as shown.

   i) Why is this done?

   ii) Copy the diagram and complete it to show how the poles of the lower magnet should be arranged.

b) The iron rods become induced magnets when placed as shown in the diagram below. Copy the diagram, and add labels to show the magnetic polarity (N or S) of the ends of both rods.

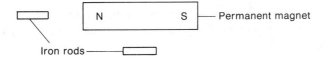

2 The bar magnet shown below is cut into two equal lengths, and each of these is divided again so that there are four pieces. Copy the diagram and add labels to show the magnetic poles (N or S) of each of the six smaller magnets.

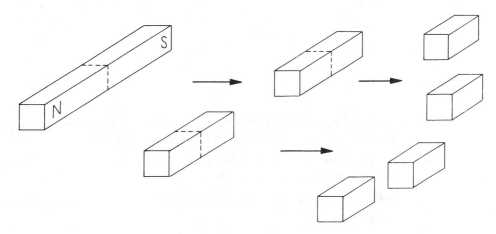

Electromagnetic Effects

1

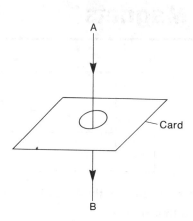

Card

a) An electric current is flowing through the wire AB. Some iron filings are sprinkled on the card, which is then tapped gently. Draw the diagram showing the pattern you would expect to see in the iron filings.

b) Name a metal which would not show this pattern when its filings are placed on the card.

2   When a current is passed through the coil, the compass needle at point X points in the direction shown. The direction of magnetic north is as indicated.

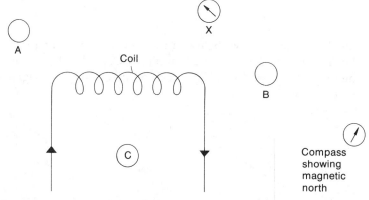

Compass
showing
magnetic
north

a) Copy the diagram and draw in the direction of the compass needles at positions A, B and C, when a current is flowing through the coil.

b) Indicate on your diagram the new direction of the compass needle at position A when the current is switched off.

c) Add labels N and S to your diagram to show the magnetic polarity of each end of the coil.

3 The diagram below shows the main parts of a meter designed to measure electric current. there are two iron bars inside a coil. one bar is fixed and the other is on the end of a pivoted pointer.

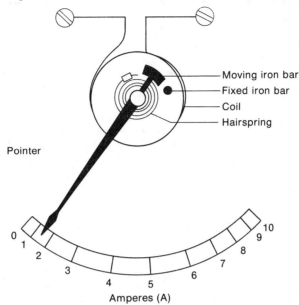

a) i) Apart from heat, what will be produced inside the coil when electricity passes through it?

   ii) Explain what effects this will have on the two iron bars.

b) What does the hairspring do?

4 a) Copy the diagram of an electromagnet. Replace the letters A–D with correct labels chosen from the list below.

   cell   soft iron core   solenoid   magnetic field lines

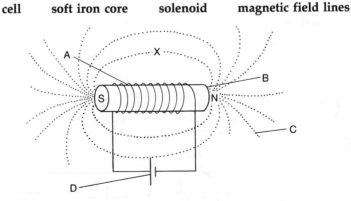

b) Add a compass to your diagram at point X, showing the direction in which the needle would point.

c) Give three ways of increasing the magnetic field strength of the electromagnet.

d) Describe one industrial use of electromagnets.

Switches and Relays

1

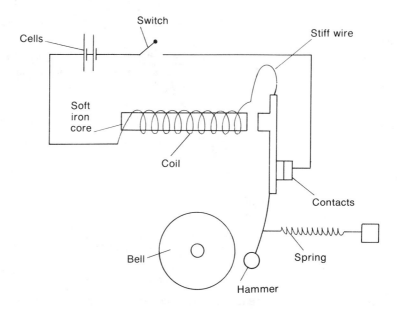

The diagram shows an electric bell. When the switch is closed, the hammer strikes the bell repeatedly.

a)   Explain why the hammer strikes the bell when the switch is closed.

b)   What is the purpose of the spring?

c)   Explain why a soft iron core is used.

2   The diagram below shows a reed switch. When a permanent magnet is placed next to the capsule, the reeds attract and the switch closes.

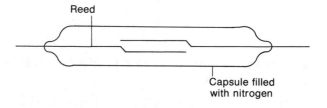

a)   Why is the capsule filled with nitrogen?

b)   Will the reed switch close if a permanent magnet is placed next to it as shown in the diagram below? Explain your answer.

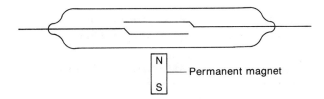

c)   The diagram shows how a reed switch can be used as a safety device for a microwave oven. Explain how the device works.

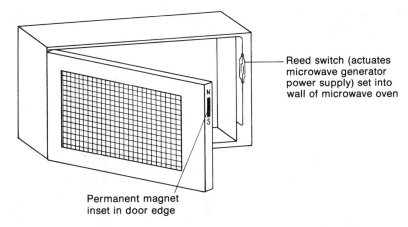

3   A lift in a tall building needs a very powerful electric motor to move it. The diagram below shows an arrangement which is used to switch the electric motor on and off.

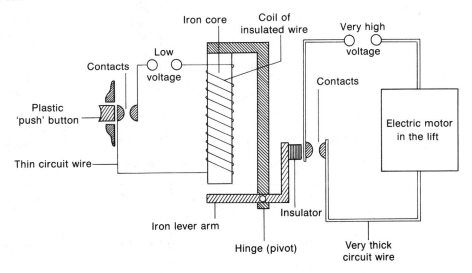

a)   Name *one* substance which would be suitable for the circuit wire.

b) What can you see in the diagram that shows the electric motor is switched *off*? Explain your answer.

c) Carefully explain how an electric current flowing through the coil of insulated wire causes the electric motor to switch on.

d) Explain why this method of switching the motor on is safer than a single simple switch in the electric motor circuit.

4 The diagram below shows a relay, operated by an electromagnet, which is used to switch on a motor.

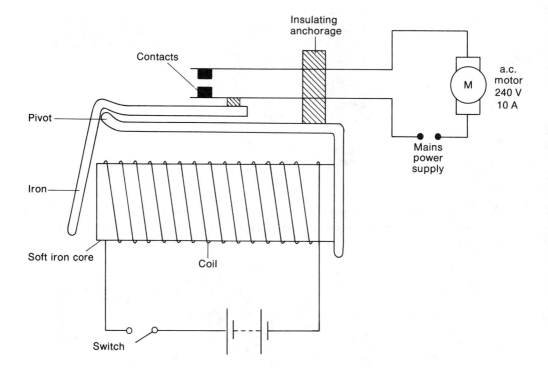

a) i) Explain why the core is made from soft iron.

ii) Suggest a suitable material for the insulating anchorage.

b) List the sequence of events which take place, from the moment the switch is closed, to the time when the motor starts.

c) i) What is the advantage of switching on the motor using a relay in this way?

ii) Suggest one practical application of this system.

5 The diagram below shows a small mammal trap, which has its own d.c. power supply.

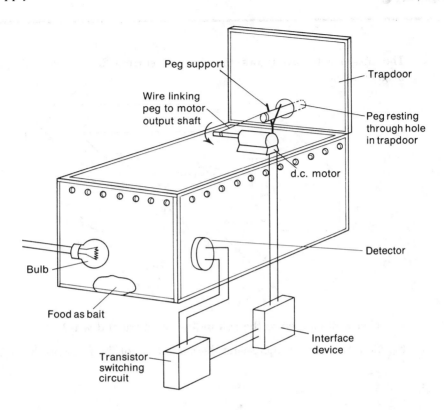

Peg support

Wire linking peg to motor output shaft

Trapdoor

Peg resting through hole in trapdoor

d.c. motor

Bulb

Detector

Food as bait

Transistor switching circuit

Interface device

a) Suggest a suitable material for making the container for the trap. Give reasons for your answer.

b) Name a suitable detector for the trap.

c) Name a suitable interface device.

d) Devise a method of switching the motor off once the peg has been removed and the trapdoor has fallen. Explain how your method works.

Motors

1 The diagram below shows the flow of current in a wire coil placed in a magnetic field.

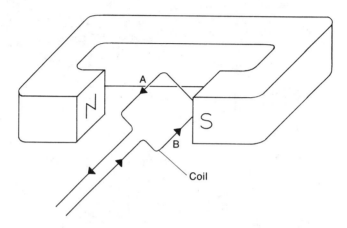

a) What will happen to the coil in this situation, and why?

b) Give *two* ways of increasing the magnitude of the force on the coil.

2

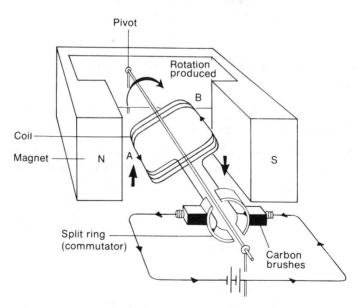

The d.c. motor shown above has a continuously rotating coil, as the split ring commutator reverses the direction of the current in the coil every half turn. The force on each of the coil segments A and B changes direction from one side of the magnet to the other.

a) Give *two* reasons why graphite (carbon) is a good choice of material for the brushes.

b) The motion of this device is jerky and it produces a small turning effect.

How would each of the following modifications improve the motor's performance? Copy and complete the table below to show how the modifications listed would improve the motor's performance.

Modification	*Improvement produced*
Several coils are used Each coil has many tens of turns The pole pieces are curved	

c) If the cell in the diagram was replaced by a sensitive, centre-zero ammeter, and the coil rotated by hand, what would the meter show when the coil began to rotate?

The Dynamo

1

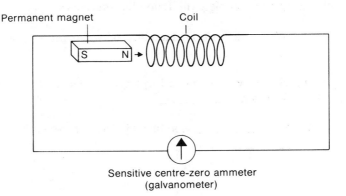

Permanent magnet   Coil

Sensitive centre-zero ammeter
(galvanometer)

When the permanent magnet is moved into the coil as shown, the galvanometer kicks to the right. What would you expect to see on the galvanometer in the following situations?

a) While removing the magnet from the coil to its starting position.

b) The magnet is turned round and the south pole is inserted into the coil.

c) The north pole of a stronger magnet is inserted as shown.

d) The magnet is stationary inside the coil.

2   A sensitive, centre-zero ammeter (galvanometer) is connected into a closed loop of wire as shown in the diagram. One section (XY) of the coil is then placed between the poles of a permanent magnet.

a) Copy the diagram below.

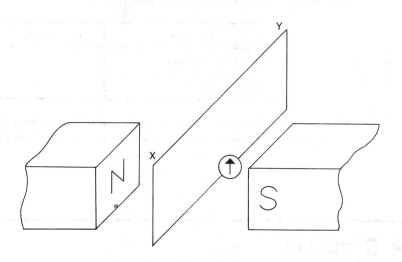

b) Copy and complete the following sentences.

i) When the wire is stationary between the magnets, the meter reading is _____.

ii) As the wire is moved upwards between the magnets, the meter needle shows a _____.

iii) An _____ is induced in the wire when it is moving in the magnetic _____.

3 The diagram shows a simple dynamo.

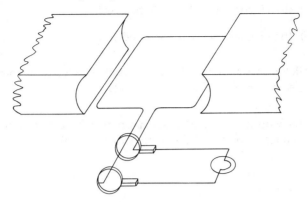

a) i) Copy the diagram and add the following labels: Permanent magnet 1, Permanent magnet 2, Bulb, Coil, Brushes, Slip rings.

ii) Using this diagram explain very briefly how the dynamo produces a current which makes the bulb light up.

b) A dynamo changes energy from one form to another. Copy and complete the diagram to show the main energy changes connected with a dynamo.

_____ energy ⟶ Dynamo ⟶ _____ energy

Transformers

1 Two coils are placed close together as shown. One has a soft iron core, and is part of an electromagnet. The other is connected to a sensitive centre-zero ammeter (galvanometer).

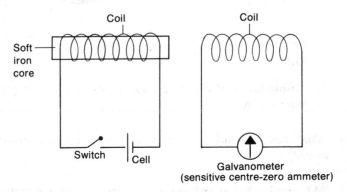

a) Copy the diagram and draw in the magnetic field lines of the electromagnet.

b) What will the galvanometer show as

    i) the electromagnet is switched on?

    ii) the electromagnet is switched off?

c) Will the meter show a deflection after the electromagnet has been switched on for some time? Explain your answer.

d) What would you expect to see happen in this experiment if the cell was replaced by an a.c. supply and the switch was closed?

2 The diagram below shows two C-cores in contact. Two coils, each of 120 turns, are placed around the cores. One coil is connected to a 4 V a.c. power supply, the other to a 6 V bulb.

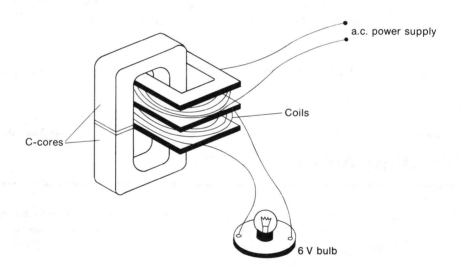

a) i) When the a.c. power supply is switched on, what would happen to the bulb?

    ii) Would the same result be obtained using a 4 V d.c. power supply? Explain your answer.

b) What change would you expect to see if the coil connected to the bulb had 180 turns?

c) At the end of the experiment the C-cores were warmer than at the start. Why is this?

3 The diagram below shows a step-up transformer.

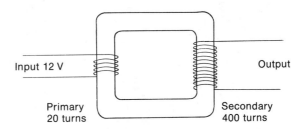

Input 12 V   Output

Primary   Secondary
20 turns   400 turns

a) Would you expect the current flowing in the coils to be a.c. or d.c.?

b) What is the output voltage?

c)   i) Give *two* reasons why a transformer such as this will not be 100% efficient.

  ii) How are modern transformers constructed to reduce the losses?

d) Draw the standard symbol for a transformer using this example.

Theme 6

Electronics

1 BASIC COMPONENTS

1 A resistor has four coloured bands as shown in the diagram.

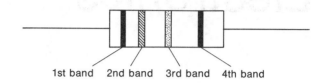

1st band   2nd band   3rd band   4th band

a) What information is obtained from the first two bands?

b) What does the third band signify?

c) The fourth band is usually silver or gold. Explain what each of these colours indicates.

d) What is the value of each of the following resistors? Consult a copy of the colour code for resistors if you cannot remember it.

	First band	Second band	Third band	Fourth band
i)	red	red	black	silver
ii)	orange	white	brown	gold
iii)	brown	black	red	gold
iv)	orange	white	orange	gold
v)	red	violet	yellow	gold

e) What are the minimum and maximum values of the resistor in d) part v)?

2 Circuit diagrams often give resistor values in the BS 1852 code. What are the values of the following resistors, expressed in this code?

a) 6K8M

b) R47K

c) 5R6J

3 a) Miniaturisation has allowed entire circuits to be constructed on a wafer of silicon small enough to pass through the eye of a needle. Other than resistors, what *three* fundamental components would you expect to find on such a circuit?

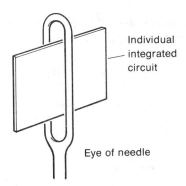

Individual integrated circuit

Eye of needle

b) Moore's law, formulated in 1960, states that the number of components that would be integrated on a single chip would double every year. If in 1970 a chip could hold 100 components, and assuming Moore's law is valid, calculate the number of components which will be integrated on a single silicon chip in the year 2000.

4 a)   i) What does the direction of the arrow in the symbol for a diode indicate?

ii) In which of the following circuits will the bulb light up when the switch is closed?

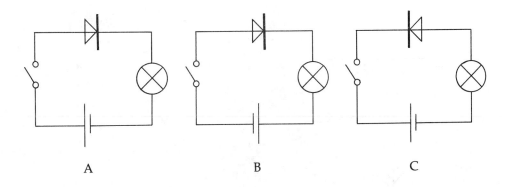

A   B   C

b) Describe *one* application of the diode in electronics.

5 Copy and complete the following table, which lists the symbols of common components together with their name.

Symbol   *Name of component*

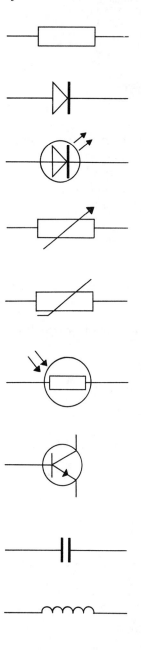

6   The graph shows how the current flowing through a semiconductor diode changes as the voltage across its ends increases.

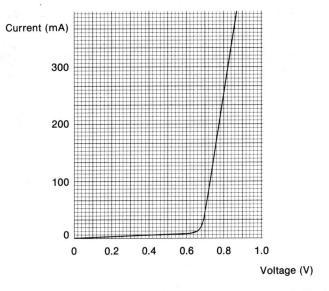

a)   i) At what applied voltage does the diode begin to conduct significantly?

   ii) What is the current flowing through the diode at an applied voltage of 0.8 V?

b)   Describe the behaviour of the diode.

c)   i) Sketch the graph of current against voltage that you would expect to obtain if the connections to the diode were interchanged.

   ii) Sketch another graph to show the behaviour of an *ideal* diode.

2 APPLICATIONS

1 The circuit shown below is used on a bicycle which has both batteries and a dynamo to power the lights. The diodes conduct only when the applied voltage exceeds 0.5 V.

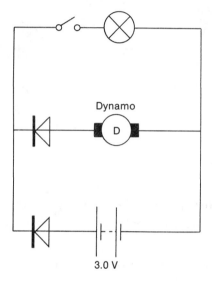

a) Give one advantage and one disadvantage of using a dynamo in place of batteries.

b) Explain how this circuit prolongs the life of the batteries.

2 Four diodes are arranged in a bridge circuit as shown below. Oscilloscopes are connected across the input and output terminals.

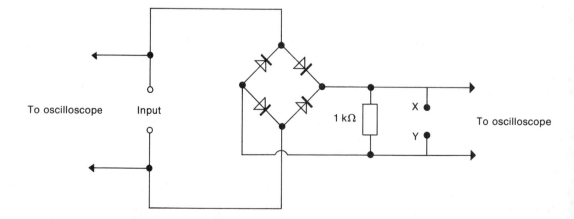

a)   The trace on the screen of the input oscilloscope is shown below. Draw a similar diagram showing the trace you would expect to see on the screen of the output oscilloscope, which has identical gain and time base settings.

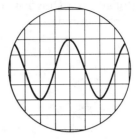

b)   A smoothing capacitor is connected between the contacts X and Y. Sketch the trace which would be seen on the screen of the output oscilloscope.

3   X is a probe which can be connected to contact A or B. Copy the circuit diagram and explain how it can be used to demonstrate the use of a transistor as a switch.

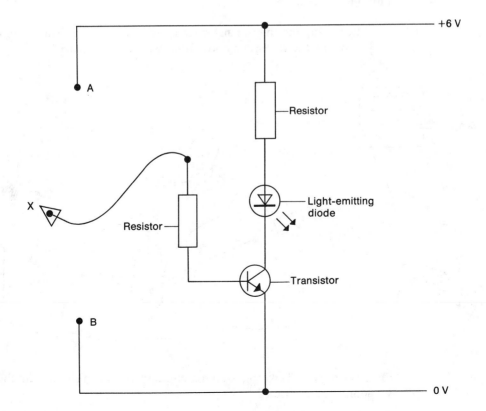

4 a) Which of the following elements can be used to make transistors?

        silicon   **iron**   **boron**   **germanium**   **carbon**

   b) Copy the transistor symbols shown below and add the labels **base, collector** and **emitter** to the correct terminals.

                     npn transistor   **pnp transistor**

5 The circuit drawn below can be used as a rain detector. When it rains, water falls on the sensor and the bulb lights up.

   a) Draw a diagram of the circuit using the correct symbol for each of the components A–E.

   b)   i) When soldering the transistor leads, Ann placed a crocodile clip on each, just below the transistor body. Why was this necessary?

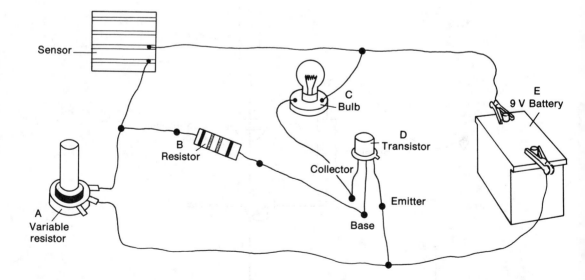

         ii) Explain why it is wrong to solder components into a circuit with the battery connected up.

c) Copy and complete the flow diagram to show which component in the circuit provides each stage in the alarm system.

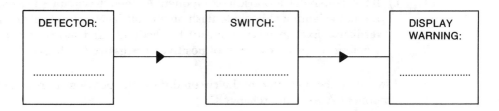

DETECTOR:

....

SWITCH:

....

DISPLAY WARNING:

....

d) Write out the passage below, inserting the missing words.

The transistor in the circuit is biased using a _____ divider, which consists of a variable resistor together with the _____. When the _____ is dry, no current flows into the _____ of the transistor and the bulb is _____. When it is raining, the _____ becomes a conductor and now the current flowing into the _____ of the transistor causes a current to flow between the _____ and _____, and the bulb is _____. The transistor is acting as a _____.

e) Suggest one use for this circuit inside the home.

6 The circuit opposite can be used to switch on a bulb automatically in the dark.

a) On a copy of the circuit, label clearly the components which are acting as a potential divider.

b) Name components A and B.

c) What is the purpose of the variable resistor R_1?

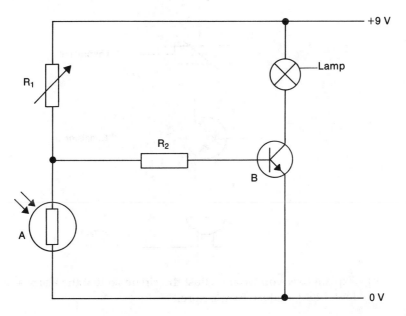

d)   i) Describe how the circuit operates. Give your answer as a sequence of events.

   ii) If the lamp is placed close to component A when the circuit is in a darkened room, the lamp will begin to flash on and off. This is due to a condition of **feedback**. Explain what is meant by feedback, and state (with reasons) whether this is an example of **positive** or **negative feedback**.

e)   How would the operation of the circuit differ if the positions of resistor R_1 and component A were interchanged?

7   During wine making, the fermenting solution must be kept at a constant temperature for best results.

a)   Draw a circuit, using the components listed below, that will sound an alarm if the solution becomes too cold.

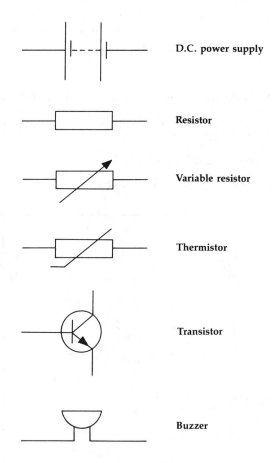

D.C. power supply

Resistor

Variable resistor

Thermistor

Transistor

Buzzer

b)   Explain how you would adjust the circuit so that the alarm sounds at a slightly lower temperature than before.

8 The diagram below shows an op amp used as an inverting amplifier

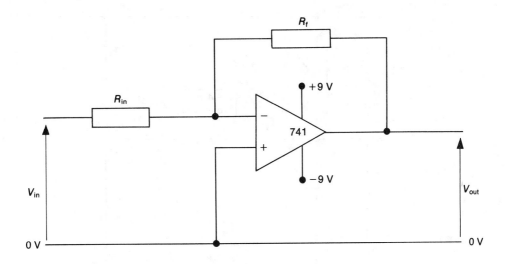

a) i) What happens to the output voltage (V_{out}) as the input voltage (V_{in}) becomes more positive?

ii) In some situations it is possible for the output of the op amp to go into saturation. What is meant by saturation?

b) What is the purpose of the resistor R_f?

c) Calculate the voltage gain when $R_f = 10\,k\Omega$, $R_{in} = 2\,k\Omega$.

d) What would V_{out} be if $R_f = 100\,k\Omega$, $R_{in} = 2\,k\Omega$ and $V_{in} = -1\,V$?

e) Copy and complete the following table by calculating the missing values.

V_{in}	R_{in}	R_f	V_{out}
+100 mV	10 kΩ	100 kΩ	
+10 mV		250 kΩ	−150 mV
−2.5 mV	10 kΩ		+2.5 V
	10 kΩ	1 MΩ	+7.5 V

9 The diagram shows a time delay circuit which includes an op amp.

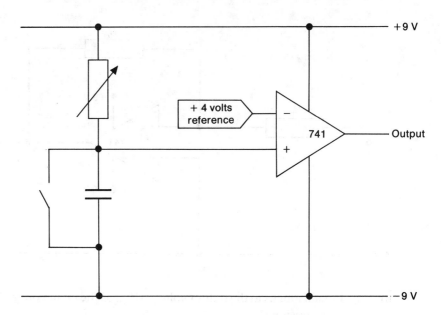

a) Describe, in simple terms, how the time delay circuit operates.

b) What would be the effect of an increase in the value of the capacitance on the length of the time delay?

c) What adjustment must be made to the variable resistor to increase the length of the time delay?

3 ELECTRONIC LOGIC

Switches and Circuits

1 The diagram below shows a simple circuit involving a switch, cell and lamp. With 0 representing 'switch open' or 'lamp off', and 1 meaning 'switch closed' or 'lamp on', the two states of the circuit can be listed in table form:

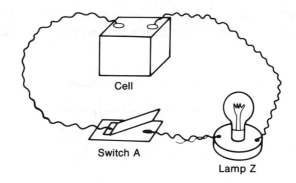

Cell

Switch A

Lamp Z

Result table

Switch A	Lamp Z
Open	Off
Closed	On

Truth table

Input A	Output Z
0	0
1	1

Construct truth tables like the one above for the following circuits, each involving two switches. Make sure you cover all combinations.

a)

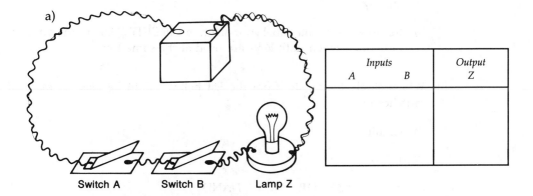

Switch A   Switch B   Lamp Z

Inputs		Output
A	B	Z

b)

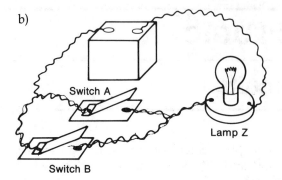

Inputs		Output
A	*B*	*Z*

2 The safe in a bank has two electronic switches, each operated by a key. When the correct keys are used, an electric current flows in the circuit and opens the lock to the safe.

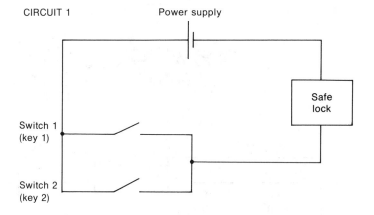

a) The bank manager wants to improve security at the bank by making it more difficult to open the safe.

   i) How many of the keys are needed to open the safe using circuit 1 as shown above?

   ii) Re-draw the circuit (label your diagram CIRCUIT 2) so that the safe lock will only open when both keys are used at the same time?

b) Which single logic gate, from the list below, could be used in place of the switches in

   i) circuit 1?

   ii) circuit 2?

AND   OR   NOT   NAND

Logic Gates

1 a) Match the following *types* of logic gate with the correct *symbol*.

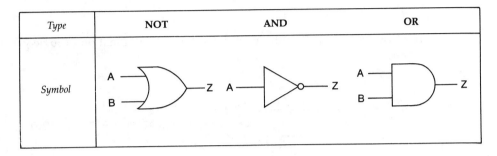

Type	NOT	AND	OR
Symbol			

b) Copy and complete the following truth tables for each named logic gate.

i) AND

Inputs		Output
A	B	Z
0	0	0
0	1	
1	0	
1	1	

ii) NAND

Inputs		Output
A	B	Z
0	0	
0	1	1
1	0	
1	1	0

iii) NOR

Inputs		Output
A	B	Z
0	0	
0	1	0
1	0	
1	1	0

2 a) In which type(s) of logic gate is

  i) the output *on* (1) when both inputs are *on* (1)?

  ii) the output *off* (0) when both inputs are *off* (0)?

  iii) the output *on* (1) when only one of the inputs is *on* (1)?

  b) Copy and complete the truth table for the combination of logic gates shown below.

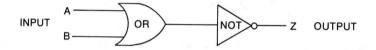

Inputs		Output
A	B	Z
0	0	
0	1	
1	0	
1	1	

  c) Draw a simpler version of the logic circuit underneath the completed truth table.

Sense and Control

1 Draw a circuit diagram to show how you would use a suitable logic gate or combination of logic gates to switch on a greenhouse heater automatically when the temperature falls below a certain level at night. Underneath your circuit diagram, explain briefly how it works.

2 A student designed a circuit for a fire alarm. It is shown in the diagram below.

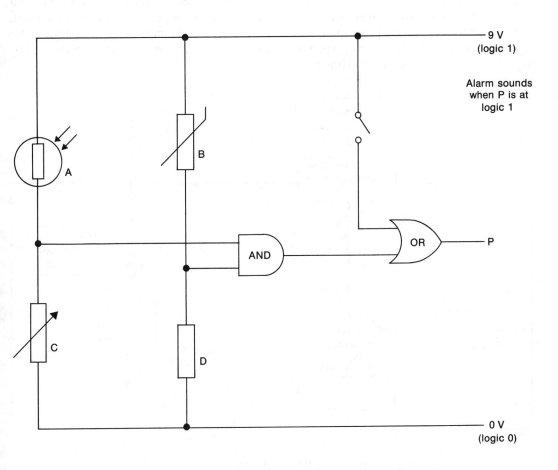

a) Copy the circuit and label the components A–D. Select labels from the following list:

      switch   **resistor**   **variable resistor**   **cell**   **thermistor**
      lamp   **diode**   **light-dependent resistor**   **light-emitting diode**

b) Which logic gate (or gates) in the circuit is (are) responsible for the fact that:

    i) the alarm sounds when a settee is burning vigorously, but not when a light is turned on in the room?

    ii) the switch can be used to test the alarm in a cold, dark room?

c) Explain why this alarm might fail to sound when there is a fire. Assume that there is no electrical fault.

3 A chicken farmer breeds chickens all the year round. His hatching shed must be kept within a few degrees of the correct temperature. There are two methods of controlling the temperature – a cold air blower and a convector heater. Both are controlled by a computer which receives information from a temperature sensor in the shed. The computer is programmed to maintain the correct temperature by operating the blower and heater in response to data from the sensor. A flow diagram for the operating program is shown below.

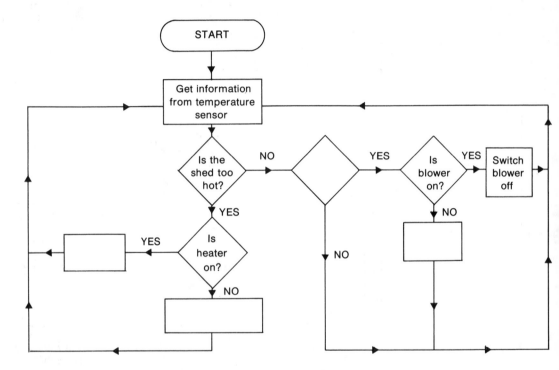

a) Copy and complete the flow diagram.

b) Name an electronic component which could be used to sense the temperature in the shed.

c) This method of controlling the temperature depends on **feedback**. Explain what is meant by feedback.

d) Give one advantage and one disadvantage of an automatic control system such as this.

4 INFORMATION HANDLING

Storing and Processing Information

1 a) List four devices used to store information. For each, state the form in which the information is stored.

b) Describe the use in everyday life of any two devices which use microelectronic components.

2 a) Explain the difference between information in **analogue** form and **digital** form.

b) ii) Describe two situations where information received by a person is in digital form.

ii) Describe two situations where information received by a person is in analogue form.

c) State *one* advantage and *one* disadvantage of transmitting information in digital form.

d) The block diagram below shows the features of an information transmission system, such as that used to send a message from one computer to another.

i) Copy the diagram.

ii) Name *one* input device which can be used to put information into a micro-computer.

iii) Name *two* output devices which allow users to obtain information from a microcomputer.

3 To convert the continuous, analogue signal shown below to digital form, sample measurements must be taken at regular intervals. This must be done sufficiently frequently to give an accurate representation of the changing analogue signal. The analogue values are digitised by assigning a binary code to each. Once in digital form, the information can be processed, stored or transmitted as required.

a) i) Copy and complete the following table, which shows the conversion of the analogue signal to digital form.

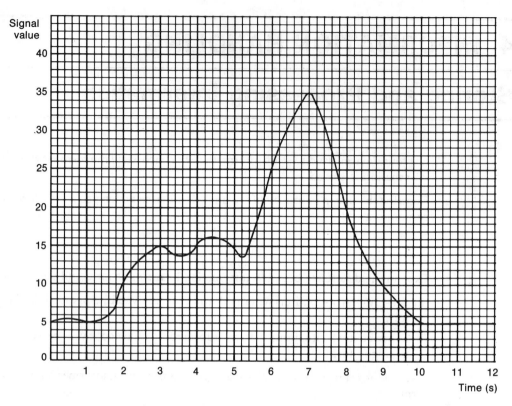

Sample time	Signal decimal value	Binary signal value (8 bit)
1	5	00000101
2	10	00001010
3		
4		
5		
6		
7		
8		
9		
10		
11		
12		

ii) Is the sampling frequency adequate? Explain your answer.

b) Devise a method of converting the letters of your first name into 8 bit binary code.

4 a) Computers are widely used in hospitals as part of patient-monitoring systems, and to help with record keeping. For instance, heart rate can be monitored by a computer in a life-support system.

i) Suggest *two* other pieces of information about a patient's condition which could be monitored by computer.

ii) Give *two* advantages which computers have over humans in life-support systems.

iii) List *two* tasks which medical staff can perform better than a computer.

b) Describe how information held on a computer could be used by a doctor to help diagnose an illness.

c) What problems can arise from keeping hospital records on a computer?

d) List *two* benefits arising from the computerisation of hospital records.

5 A **bistable** or 'flip-flop' is a logic circuit which is used to store the binary data in the central processing unit of computers. The following diagram shows a bistable, constructed by cross-coupling two NOR gates.

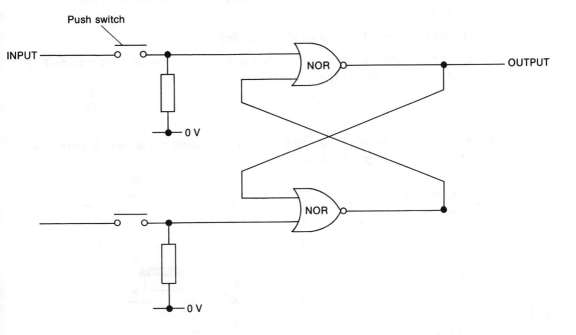

a) What must happen to cause the bistable to revert to its original state following an input signal?

b) It is said that the device 'remembers' that an input has been made. Explain what this means by describing the operation of the bistable. You should assume that the output is at logic 1 initially.

c) i) What name is given to a bistable with only one of its outputs in use, like that shown in the diagram?

ii) What term is used to describe a set of bistables linked together to store data?

6 Optical fibres, made of very pure glass, can be used in transmitting telephone calls as shown in the flow diagram below. More calls can be transmitted using these fibres than when conventional cables of a similar diameter are used.

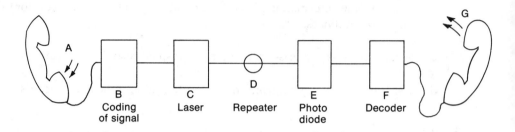

a) Briefly explain what is happening at each stage A–G.

b) Between which stages in the sequence is the information transmitted using optical fibres?

c) What is a repeater and why is it needed?

d) Why are telephone conversations transmitted using optical fibres more difficult to 'tap', and therefore more secure?

7 The diagram below shows a simple radio receiver built by a student. It incorporates a ZN414 radio integrated circuit.

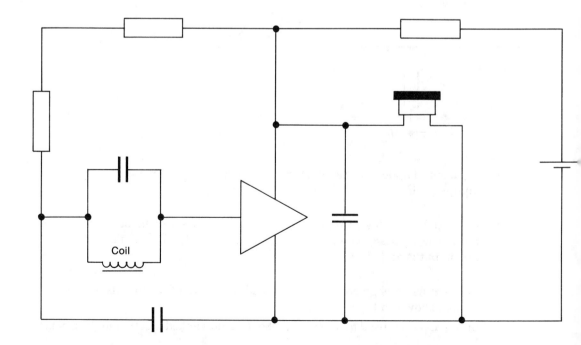

The coil is made by wrapping 50 turns of thin copper wire around a small cardboard tube. A 10 cm ferrite rod is then placed inside the coil. The radio can be tuned by slowly pushing the rod in or out of the coil.

a)   i) Copy the circuit diagram, and add the following labels at the correct positions. Some may need to be used more than once.

    cell   **integrated circuit**   **earphone**   **capacitor**   **resistor**

    ii) Suggest one operation carried out by the integrated circuit.

b)   Given a list of radio programmes and the wavelength of each station, describe how you would investigate how the wavelength of the radio waves received depends on the length of rod inside the coil.

c)   An alternative method of tuning the circuit involves replacing one of the capacitors by a **variable capacitor**. Indicate clearly on your diagram which capacitor should be replaced.

Communicating Information

1

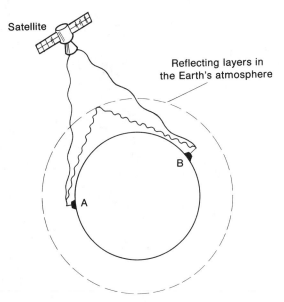

Communication between stations at points A and B on the Earth's surface can take place using short wave radio signals (wavelength 10–100 m, frequency 3–30 MHz) or a via a satellite link using microwaves (wavelength 0.1–0.01 m, frequency 3–30 GHz).

(1 MHz = 10^6 Hz, 1 GHz = 10^9 Hz)

a) What prevents the use of microwaves for long-distance communication on the Earth's surface?

b) Why are microwaves needed for communication via satellite?

c) List *two* advantages of microwave links which arise through the high frequency of the radiation used.

d) Describe *one* application of microwaves in the home, and any hazards associated with their use.

2 In approximately 750 words, discuss the impact which modern information technology has had on our lives. You should mention data storage systems, data processing and communication of information in your answer.

Theme 7

Earth and
Space

1 ATMOSPHERE

Local Weather

1   The following symbols are used on weather maps and charts. Explain what each symbol represents.

a)

b)

c)   LOW

d)

e)

f)

2   Kalpesh recorded the temperature on one day every week for a year. The readings
were taken at midday, and were used to calculate the mean (average) temperature
for each month as shown in the table below.

Month	Mean temperature (°C)
January	−2.0
February	+2.5
March	+6.0
April	+10.0
May	+14.0
June	+16.5
July	+20.0
August	+19.0
September	+14.5
October	+10.5
November	+5.0
December	+1.5

a)   i) Use the results in the table to plot a column graph showing the temperature
variation over the year.

ii) Does Kalpesh live in the northern or southern hemisphere? Explain your
answer.

b)   Alan, another of the students in Kalpesh's class, carried out similar measurements and produced the following bar graph.

Mean temperature (°C)

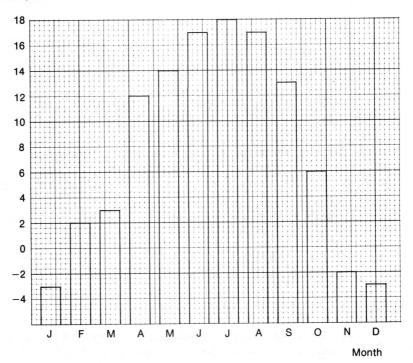

Month

      i) Explain why Alan's readings can be different to Kalpesh's without being wrong.

      ii) How could the accuracy of both sets of results be improved?

c)   Copy and complete the following table.

	Kalpesh	*Alan*
Month with the highest mean temperature		
Month with the lowest mean temperature		
Mean temperature for the whole year		

3

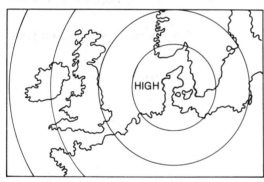 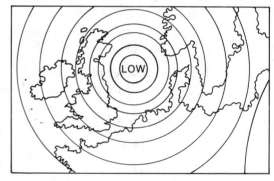

10 June   5 December

The two weather maps show the isobar pattern over north-west Europe at two different times of year. All other symbols (except HIGH and LOW) have been removed.

a)   What does an isobar represent?

b)   In each case, predict the direction and strength of the winds over Great Britain.

c)   Using the information on the maps, describe the weather conditions in Britain on
      i) 10 June
      ii) 5 December

4 a)   Explain the difference between climate and weather.

    b)   The climate graphs following are for different places in the world. Look at the graphs and answer the questions which follow.

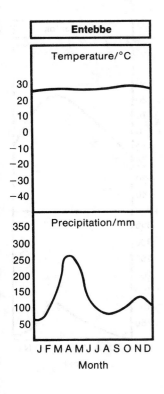

Entebbe

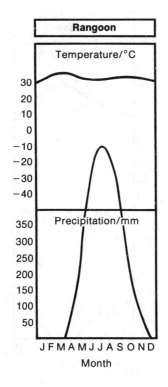

Rangoon

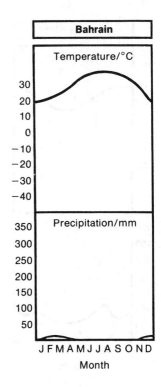

Bahrain

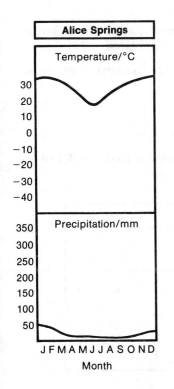

Alice Springs

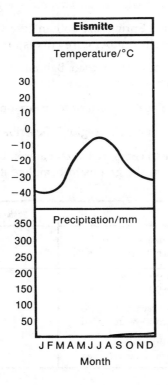

Eismitte

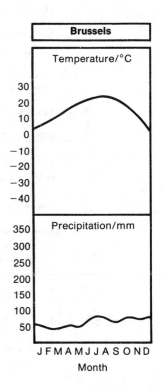

Brussels

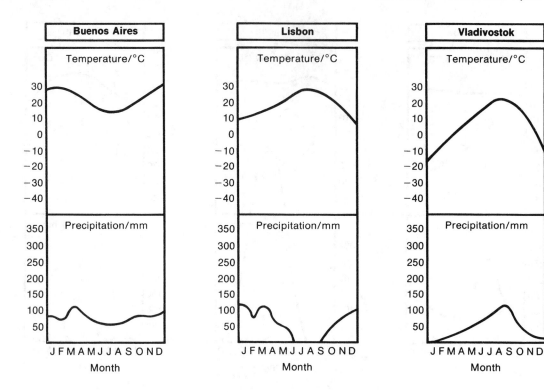

i) Which of the places is closest to the equator? Describe one feature of the climate which is typical of an equatorial region.

ii) Bahrain and Alice Springs are both in desert regions. Explain the difference in the shape of the temperature curves for the two places.

iii) Which two places (other than Bahrain and Alice Springs) have similar climates to each other?

iv) Which of the places has a monsoon season?

v) Which place is in a polar region? Describe its climate.

vi) Copy this table to compare the climates in Lisbon and Vladivostok and use information from the graphs to complete it.

	Lisbon	Vladivostok
Highest temperature recorded Month in which it was recorded		
Lowest temperature recorded Month in which it was recorded		
Highest rainfall recorded Month in which it was recorded		
Lowest rainfall recorded Month in which it was recorded		

5   The diagram shows the paths of four airstreams which flow over Britain in the summer.

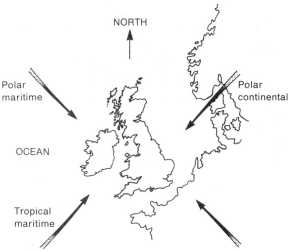

a)   Copy or trace the diagram and add the name of the fourth (missing) airstream.

b)   Suggest the similarity in the types of weather brought by the polar maritime and the tropical maritime airstreams.

c)   Which airstream will bring colder, drier weather?

6   Read the passage below. Use the information in the passage and your knowledge to answer the questions which follow.

> Over lengthy periods climate can change. A long-term shift of only 1 °C is enough to trigger such profound changes as the Little Ice Age in Western Europe, which peaked in the late 17th century. A drop of 4 °C is enough to bring on a full ice age. At the moment we are in one of the warmest phases of the past 1000 years. (In the northern hemisphere between 1881 and 1983, the warmest year was 1981.)
>
> Climatic change is the norm. The one thing that we can be sure about with regard to future climate is that it will feature deep-seated shifts, even if we leave it to get on with its own natural course – without disrupting it by, for example, contributing to carbon dioxide build-up in the atmosphere. This has major implications for our capacity to keep producing food. Throughout the world, climate is a critical factor in agriculture. During the late 1960s, the drought in the Sahel brought disaster to entire nations. In 1972 another drought inflicted such damage on the Soviet wheat crop that it helped to quadruple world prices within two years. In 1974, a delayed monsoon in India wrought havoc for millions of people. In 1975 pulses of cold air ravaged Brazil's coffee crop, causing inflationary upheavals in coffee prices around the world.
>
> Conversely, of course, a stable climate, or rather a climate with slow and predictable change, can be a tremendous asset that can basically enrich our lives.
>
> *Adapted from* Gaia Atlas of Planet Management.

a)   Explain why 'climate is a critical factor in agriculture'.

b) i) How are we 'contributing to carbon dioxide build-up in the atmosphere'?

    ii) What effect is this build-up likely to have on the Earth's climate?

c) i) What happened to coffee prices in 1976?

    ii) Explain why this happened.

d) In recent years there have been droughts in Ethiopia and the Sudan. What was the effect on the people living in these areas?

e) What is meant by a 'stable climate'?

f) Why do you think the author describes a stable climate as 'a tremendous asset'?

7

Day: on-shore breeze   **Night: off-shore breeze**

The diagrams show the direction of coastal breezes by day and night.

a) Copy the diagrams.

b) Below are some statements about coastal breezes. Make a copy of the table below. Consider each pair of statements and decide which one goes into which column in the following table, then write in the statements.

During the day	During the night

    i) Land (rocks, soil) warms up more quickly than water/Water cools down more slowly than land.

    ii) Warmer air rises over the land/Warmer air rises over the sea.

    iii) Colder air over the land is more dense and falls/Colder air over the sea is more dense and falls.

    iv) Breezes blow from sea to land/Breezes blow from land to sea.

Global Effects

1

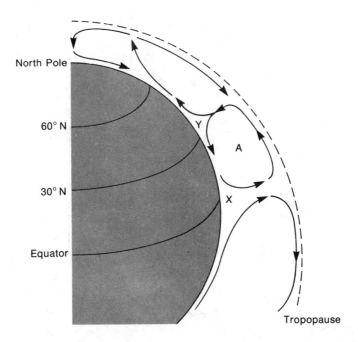

The diagram shows the movement of air between the Earth's surface and the tropopause in the northern hemisphere during April. Air rising above the equator can move in a northerly or southerly direction, returning to ground level about one-third of the way to the poles. Cold polar air descends and moves underneath warmer air from the equator. These general patterns persist throughout the year.

a) Describe how the height of the tropopause varies in the hemisphere.

b) What name is given to the transfer of heat by circulating currents like those around point A in the diagram?

c) What causes air to rise above point X on the equator?

d) Would you expect the air pressure at sea level near point X to be greater or less than that near point Y? Explain your answer.

e) The wind patterns shown in the diagram, drift north or south on a seasonal basis. Suggest an explanation for this drift.

2 The burning of fuels produces 14 000 million tonnes of carbon dioxide per year. Carbon dioxide is one of the gases in the atmosphere which allow short wavelength infra-red radiation from the Sun to pass through but which stop some of the long wavelength infra-red radiation from Earth leaving the atmosphere.

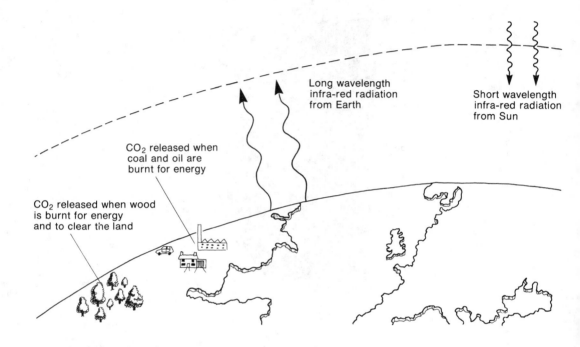

a) Why is the infra-red radiation re-emitted by the Earth of longer wavelength than that received?

b) The levels of carbon dioxide in the atmosphere are rising.

   i) What is the *main* human activity which is contributing to the increase?

   ii) Suggest and explain one other activity which may also be contributing to this increase.

c) State and explain what effect the increase in CO_2 levels could have on the

   i) climate in Britain

   ii) mean sea level

d) What effects might the changes you have described in c) have on the lives of people in Britain?

3   For each of the following changes, suggest one effect that the change would have on the surface conditions on Earth. Write out the completed table.

Change	Effect of the change on surface conditions on Earth
a) The average distance between the Sun and Earth decreases.	
b) The Sun's power output decreases.	
c) The Earth's rate of rotation decreases so that there are 265 days in one year.	
d) A series of volcanic eruptions fills the atmosphere with dust.	
e) The tilt of the Earth's axis increases from 23.5° to 28°.	

2 GEOPHYSICS

Earthquakes and Volcanoes

1

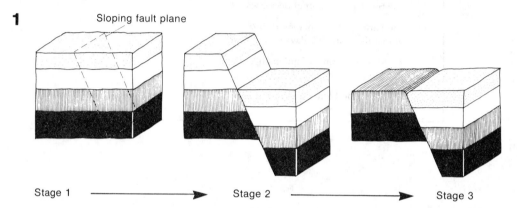

Sloping fault plane

Stage 1 ⟶ Stage 2 ⟶ Stage 3

The diagrams show three stages in the evolution of the land near a fault zone.

a) In stage 1, were the rocks on each side of the fault under compression or tension? Explain your answer.

b) Describe the changes which have occurred between stages 2 and 3, and give two possible causes.

c) Draw a diagram, equivalent to stage 3, showing one possible outcome when the forces acting on the rocks are in the opposite direction to those in this example.

d) What is the origin of the forces which caused the movement?

2

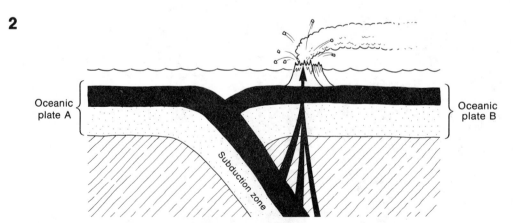

Oceanic plate A

Oceanic plate B

Subduction zone

Mobile plates in the Earth's crust collide as a result of tectonic action. At destructive plate margins, crust is forced downwards in a subduction zone. In the example shown, two oceanic plates are involved.

a) In which direction is each of the plates moving?

b) Give *two* reasons why rock forced downwards into a subduction zone is likely to melt, leading to volcanism.

c) What would be found above a subduction zone where two continental plates are colliding?

d) What is believed to be the driving force for tectonic action?

3 The article reproduced below appeared in *The Daily Telegraph* of 26th September, 1984. Read the article carefully and answer the questions which follow.

VOLCANO ASH DIMS SUNLIGHT

By IAN WARD in Manila

A SIX MILE-HIGH dense cloud of ash hung yesterday over the entire southern Luzon province of Albay, where the Mayon volcano continues its spectacular display.

Thousands fled villages threatened by flows of lava and mud.

The aerial blanket of ash transformed the noon sky over the province into a murky half-light as farmers around the volcano abandoned vast stretches of rice fields now lying under large layers of mud.

Philippine Airlines removed all jets from its southern Luzon schedules, replacing them with propeller-driven aircraft as a safety precaution against airborne volcanic ash, which can quickly snuff out jet engines.

Boulders big as cars

The Philippine Civil Aviation Authority continued to warn foreign commercial aircraft to fly clear of the ash clouds, which were drifting in several directions from the erupting crater, but have been meticulously plotted by satellite technology.

Throughout the day Mayon hurled boulders as big as cars into the air and down its slopes. To add to the awesome display flashes of lightning repeatedly hit the top of the belching cone of the volcano.

But vulcanologists said seismic readings were now suggesting that the worst of the eruption, which began with a huge blast on September 9, was over.

Many evacuees have been treated for burns and lung problems associated with inhalation of gases and ash, but no deaths have been reported as a result of the volcano's present eruption.

a) Why did the population flee from their valleys?

b) Why were jets forbidden from flying near the volcanic eruption?

c) The eruption produced liquid, solid and gaseous materials.

   i) Name *one* solid and *one* liquid which were thrown out.

   ii) Name *one* gas which escapes from a volcano.

4   The map below shows part of the world with plate boundaries and plate movement
indicated.

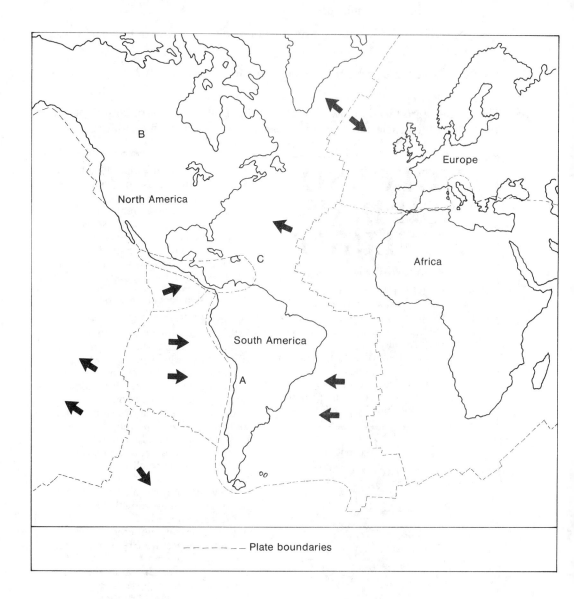

- - - - - - - Plate boundaries

a)   Trace the map and add labels to indicate one constructive and one destructive
plate margin.

b)   At which of the sites A, B or C would you expect to find
   i)   volcanism?
   ii) mountain building?

5

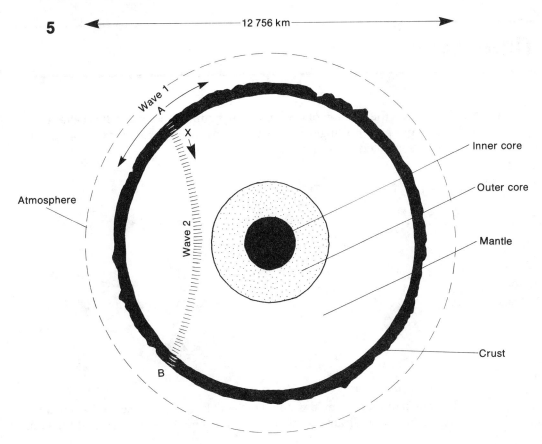

The diagram (not to scale) shows the layered internal structure of the Earth. An earthquake occurring at X, directly below the epicentre (A), is detected at location B. Shock waves arrive at B over a period of 15 minutes.

a) What name is given to point X?

b) Which wave is a P wave?

c) An earthquake occurs when forces inside the Earth cause large masses of rock to fracture and move. Waves from the Earthquake travel through the Earth and along the crust.
   i) Explain why the wave travelling through the Earth takes a curved path.
   ii) Give two reasons why waves travelling along the crust take longer to reach location B than those travelling through the mantle.
   iii) Would you expect earthquakes to originate below a depth of 1000 km? Explain your answer.

d) Suggest one result of a major earthquake occurring beneath the sea.

e) Give two pieces of information which suggest that the Earth has a core containing iron.

Timescales

1   The map shows the location of two regions of granite in Scotland. It is believed that they were once part of a single granite mass. Movement of rock masses along a fault line slowly separated the two samples.

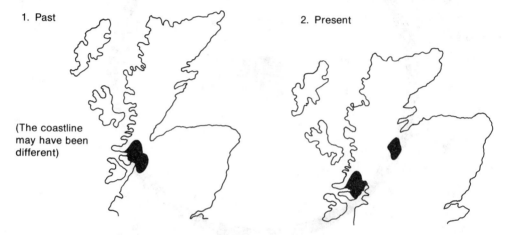

a)   Trace map number 2 and draw on it the fault line responsible for the separation. Add arrows to indicate the direction of movement on each side of the fault.

b)   Choose a timescale from those listed below in which this change is likely to have occurred.

   5 years   5000 years   5 million years

c)   The distance between the granite locations today is approximately 100 km. Using your answer to part b), calculate the average rate of displacement in centimetres per year.

d)   What causes displacements such as this?

2   Some chemical elements decay with age, producing radioactivity in the process. Potassium turns into argon, and rubidium into strontium. Uranium-238 is an element which decays through a series of radioactive products to finish as lead-206. In any uranium ore the proportion of lead-206 increases with time. The decay occurs at a constant rate, the half-life of uranium-238 being 4 500 000 000 years.

Explain briefly how scientists can use this information to determine the age of rocks.

3 ASTRONOMY

Sun, Earth and Moon

1 The following diagram shows part of the **solar system** (not to scale).

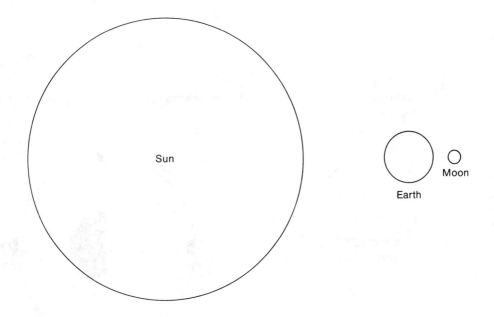

a) Which of the bodies is a **star**?

b) Why is the Moon not a **planet**?

c) Name two planets which orbit closer to the Sun than the Earth does.

d) When Columbus set sail to find the New World in 1492, people thought he would fall off the edge of the Earth. What evidence do we have that the Earth is not flat?

2 Pair these groups of words to form correct statements.

We experience day and night on Earth once every 24 hours because   the Earth's axis is tilted at $23\frac{1}{2}°$.

We see different phases of the Moon in a regular cycle because   the Earth completes one orbit of the Sun in one year.

There are seasonal changes in climate on Earth because	the Earth rotates once on its axis once in one day.
We see different constellations (star patterns) at different times of year because	the Moon rotates once on its axis in the same time that it takes to complete one orbit of the Earth.
We only ever see about one half of the Moon's surface from Earth because	the Moon orbits the Earth approximately once every 28 days.

3   The diagram below shows the Moon orbiting the Earth. Four positions in the orbit are shown.

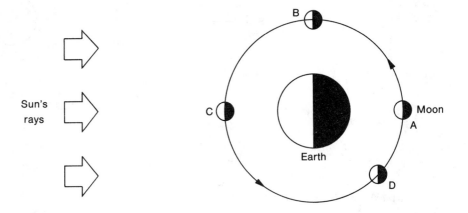

a)   The Moon has no light of its own. Explain why we can see the Moon shining in the sky.

b)   Draw and name the phases of the moon as they would be seen from a point on Earth when the Moon is at

   i) position A

   ii) position B

   iii) position D

c)   At what position must the Moon be for a total eclipse of the Sun to occur?

d)   Explain why a total eclipse of the Moon is not seen every time the Moon passes through position A.

4   a)   The diagram below shows the Earth rotating on its axis.

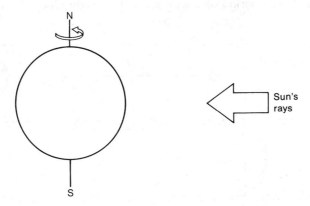

   i)   Copy the diagram, adding a line to show the boundary between day and night.

   ii)   Shade the part of the Earth shown on the diagram which is experiencing night.

   b)   The diagram below shows the Earth in orbit around the Sun.

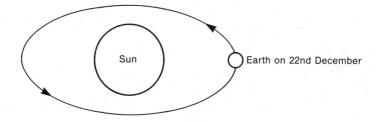

   i)   Copy the diagram and add to it the position of the Earth six months after 22nd December.

   ii)   What force keeps the earth orbiting the Sun?

5   The diagram below shows a student's log. She had been asked to draw the phase of the Moon over a period of 2 months, and had completed 1 month.

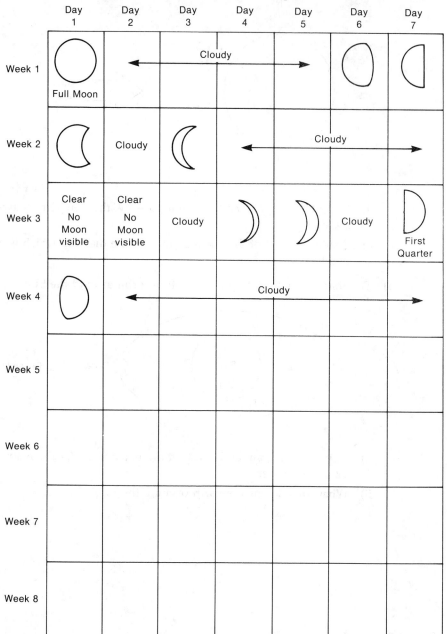

a)   Sketch the phase of the Moon she would have seen on day 1 of week 5 if the sky had been clear (no clouds).

b)   On which day in week 7 would she expect to see a **First Quarter** phase?

c)   Explain how the shape of the Moon seems to change from week to week when the sky is clear.

6 Read the passage below which is about **tides**. Answer the questions which follow.

> Much of the Earth's surface is covered with water. Because water is a fluid it can move easily in response to gravity. The gravitational pull of the Moon causes the waters to rise and fall, in most places twice very 24 hours 50 minutes. When a particular part of the Earth is in line with the Moon, the water bulges and the tide rises. As the Earth spins on its axis the bulge moves across the oceans like a giant wave. The diagram below assumes that all the Earth is covered with water to make it easier to interpret.

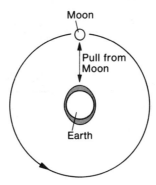

> The Sun has a similar but smaller gravitational effect. At New Moon and Full Moon both Sun and Moon are in line with the Earth. The combined effect means that the tides are at their highest and are called **spring** tides. At First and Last Quarter Moon the Sun and Moon are at right angles. The gravitational pull of the Moon is partly cancelled out by the gravitational pull of the Sun. The tides are at their lowest and are called **neap** tides.

a) What is responsible for creating the rise and fall of the tides?

b) How often is there a high tide in most places on Earth?

c) Approximately how much of the Earth's surface is actually covered with water? (You may need to use a reference book.)

d) Explain the difference between spring and neap tides.

e) Draw diagrams which show the relative positions of the Earth, oceans, Moon and Sun at

    i) spring tide at New Moon.

    ii) neap tide at First Quarter.

7 The diagram opposite, which is not drawn to scale, shows the Sun–Earth arrangement during summer and winter.

a) Which feature shown in the diagram is responsible for the seasonal changes in climate experienced on Earth?

b) By referring to the diagram, explain how the northern hemisphere experiences summer while the southern hemisphere experiences winter.

c) At midsummer in the northern hemisphere, what is the minimum latitude from which you would be able to see the Sun above the horizon for 24 hours each day?

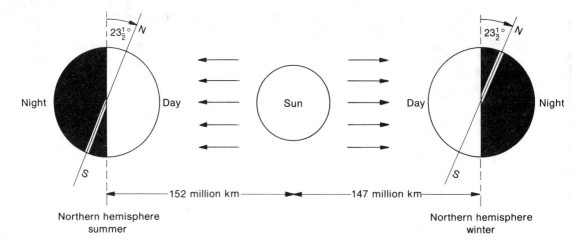

Northern hemisphere
summer

Northern hemisphere
winter

8 The diagram below, which is not to scale, shows how an eclipse of the Sun occurs when the shadow of the Moon falls on the Earth.

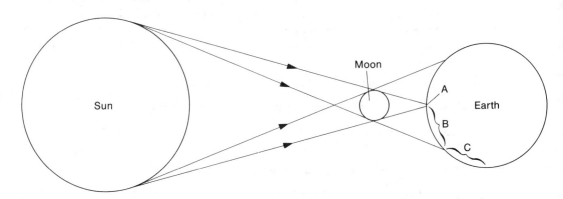

a) Copy the diagram.

b) Describe what you would see from the Earth during a total eclipse of the Sun.

c) From which of the regions A, B or C on Earth would an observer see

    i) a total eclipse of the Sun?

    ii) a partial eclipse of the Sun?

d) i) Draw a second diagram showing the Moon in a position where a suitably placed astronaut on the Moon would see a total eclipse of the Sun.

    ii) What would an observer on the night side of the Earth see when the Moon is in this position?

9   The formula for the force of attraction between two masses, m and M, with centres separated by a distance d, is

$$\text{force} = \frac{GMm}{d^2} \quad (G \text{ is the gravitational constant})$$

Use this formula to predict:

a)   the change in the force of attraction between two objects when the mass of one of them is doubled.

b)   the change in the force of attraction when the distance between the masses is doubled.

c)   the change in the force of attraction between the Earth and the Sun if the Sun collapsed to become a black hole without loss of mass.

10

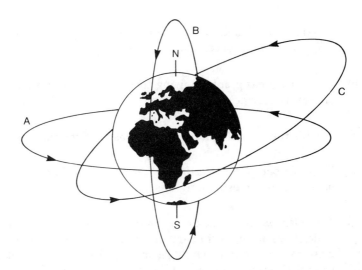

The diagram shows three satellites orbiting the Earth. One is in a geostationary orbit.

a)   Which satellite is in a polar orbit?

b)   i) Explain what is meant by a 'geostationary' orbit.
      ii) Which satellite is in a geostationary orbit?

c)   What force holds the satellites in orbit?

d)   Write down *three* different uses of satellites. In each case say how they have improved our way of life.

The Solar System

1 The following table gives the average density of the planets, listed in alphabetical order. The value for Pluto has been left out.

Planet	Density (kg/m³)
Earth	5500
Jupiter	1300
Mars	4000
Mercury	5400
Neptune	1700
Pluto	
Saturn	700
Uranus	1300
Venus	5200

a) Arrange the planets in order of increasing distance from the Sun using a reference book if necessary.

b) Construct a bar graph showing the density of the planets placed in order of increasing distance from the Sun.

c) What is the overall pattern in the density of the planets in the solar system?

d) Use your bar graph to estimate the density of Pluto. What assumption do you have to make in estimating this value?

e) The solar system can be divided into two groups of planets, the *terrestrial planets*, which have densities similar to the Earth, and the *gas giants*, which have densities close to that of water ($1000 \, kg/m^3$). Which planets would you place in each group? Give your answer in the form of a table.

f) One theory concerning the early history of the solar system states that the high temperatures close to the Sun caused volatile, low density materials to 'boil away'. These materials then 'condensed' further out from the Sun.
   i) Does this theory account for the pattern in density of the planets?
   ii) In addition to temperature, what other factor must be considered in deciding whether the gases in a planet's atmosphere can escape into space?

g) Name one other type of object in the solar system apart from the Sun and planets.

Stars

1 a)   What is the difference between a planet and a star?

b)   Explain why the apparent motion of planets in the sky is visible from night to night, yet the stars keep their positions for centuries.

c)   Give one reason, not concerned with motion, why the appearance of the night sky will be different in several million years' time.

2

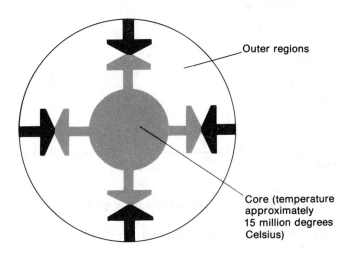

The diagram shows the balance of forces in a star such as the Sun. Outward pressure from nuclear reactions in the core balances the inward pressure from the weight of the outer regions. This balance may remain for between one million and a million million years, depending on the mass of the star. The nuclear reactions in the core occur at a greater rate as the temperature increases, and produce heavier elements (such as helium and carbon) from hydrogen. When the core hydrogen is used up, the period of stability comes to an end.

a)   What *type* of nuclear reaction takes place in the star's core?

b)   What is the force which pulls the outer regions of the star towards the centre?

c)   Which chemical element is the most common in stars like the Sun?

d)   What would happen to the outward pressure from the core if the temperature there increased?

e)   A more massive star must support the greater inward pressure from heavier outer layers. Would you expect the temperature at the core to be greater or less than that in the Sun? Explain your choice.

f)   Use the diagram to predict what happens to a star when nuclear reactions in the core stop.

g)   It is thought that the Sun can maintain this balance for around ten thousand million years. Give one piece of evidence from the passage which suggests that a more massive 'giant' star will become out of balance sooner.

3   a)   What is the difference between a **constellation** and a **star cluster**?

b)   The diagrams below show how the star pattern in the constellation Cassiopeia will change with time:

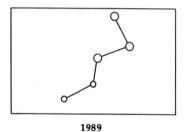      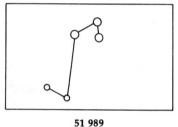

        1989   26 989   51 989

i)   What is the cause of the changing pattern?

ii)   Why does it appear to change so slowly?

Galaxies and Cosmology

1   a)   When we measure the velocities of distant galaxies by analysing light from them, they all appear to be moving away from us.

i)   What is the cause of this motion?

ii)   Using the diagram of a model universe below, explain why our Milky Way galaxy is not the centre of the universe in spite of the observation that galaxies are moving away in all directions.
(Hint: view the change from any other galaxy.)

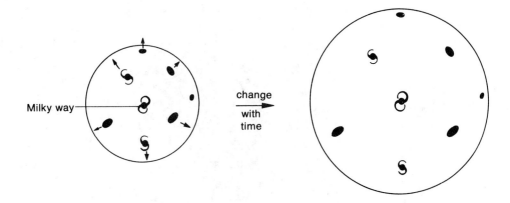

b)   What force may ultimately halt the expansion of the universe?